THE CAT NAME COMPANION

THE CAT NAME COMPANION

Facts and Fables to Help You Name Your Feline

M A R K   B R Y A N T

A Citadel Press Book
Published by Carol Publishing Group

Carol Publishing Group Edition, 1995

A Citadel Press Book
Published by Carol Publishing Group
Citadel Press is a registered trademark of Carol Communications, Inc.

Editorial Offices: 600 Madison Avenue, New York, NY 10022
Sales & Distribution Offices: 120 Enterprise Avenue, Secaucus, NJ 07094
In Canada: Canadian Manda Group, One Atlantic Avenue, Suite 105
Toronto, Ontario, M6K 3E7

Queries regarding rights and permissions should be addressed to:
Carol Publishing Group, 600 Madison Avenue, New York, NY 10022

Manufactured in the United States of America
10 9 8 7 6 5 4 3 2 1

Carol Publishing Group books are available at special discounts
for bulk purchases, sales promotions, fund raising, or
educational purposes. Special editions can also be created to
specifications. For details contact: Special Sales Department,
Carol Publishing Group, 120 Enterprise Ave., Secaucus, NJ 07094

Library of Congress Cataloging-in-Publication Data

Bryant, Mark, 1953–
    The cat name companion : facts and fables to help you name
    your feline / Mark Bryant.
        p. cm.
    "A Citadel Press book."
    ISBN 0-8065-1671-2 (pbk.)
    1. Cats—Names. I. Title.
SF442.4.B78   1995
929.97—dc20
                                                    95-19776
                                                    CIP

For
Kathleen

The Naming of Cats

The Naming of Cats is a difficult matter,
  It isn't just one of your holiday games;
You may think at first I'm as mad as a hatter
When I tell you, a cat must have THREE DIFFERENT NAMES.
First of all, there's the name that the family use daily,
  Such as Peter, Augustus, Alonzo or James,
Such as Victor or Jonathan, George or Bill Bailey —
  All of them sensible everyday names.
There are fancier names if you think they sound sweeter,
  Some for the gentlemen, some for the dames:
Such as Plato, Admetus, Electra, Demeter —
  But all of them sensible everyday names.
But I tell you, a cat needs a name that's particular,
  A name that's peculiar, and more dignified,
Else how can he keep up his tail perpendicular,
  Or spread out his whiskers, or cherish his pride?
Of names of this kind, I can give you a quorum,
  Such as Munkustrap, Quaxo, or Coricopat,
Such as Bombalurina, or else Jellylorum —
  Names that never belong to more than one cat.
But above and beyond there's still one name left over,
  And that is the name that you never will guess;
The name that no human research can discover —
  But THE CAT HIMSELF KNOWS, and will never confess.
When you notice a cat in profound meditation,
  The reason, I tell you, is always the same:
His mind is engaged in a rapt contemplation
  Of the thought, of the thought, of the thought of his name:
    His ineffable effable
    Effanineffable
Deep and inscrutable singular Name.

T.S. Eliot, Old Possum's Book of Practical Cats

Contents

Preface

This has been a maddening but delightful book to put together
— one simply doesn't know when to stop. No comprehensive
survey of historical pet-names exists so that ever more examples leap out of the woodwork daily, and I am sure readers
will know of many, many more. The problem is complicated
further when trying to find suitable descriptions of colours,
shades and patterns — not to mention those punning wit-
ticisms that can make names so entertaining. So, for all those
whose pet doesn't appear here, my apologies. You at least, for
better or for worse, have solved the problem of naming your cat,
and if you would like to share its distinction with others I will
do my best to include it in future editions. Meanwhile, for those
yet to christen their pedigree kitten, newly acquired stray or
inherited nameless moggy, I hope what follows helps to get the
furball rolling — they are only suggestions, after all.

The appearance of this book has been greatly enhanced by
the charming illustrations of Karen Daws and the thoughtful
design work of Harold King, to both of whom I owe a debt of
gratitude. I would also like to thank Jeremy Robson and Louise
Dixon of Robson Books for their patience and encouragement
in bringing this project to its final fruition.

M.B.

Introduction

Samuel Butler once said that the test of one's literary power is whether you can name a kitten. He confessed himself 'condemned' as he couldn't. In a similar vein, the T.S. Eliot poem that appears at the beginning of this book also seems to imply that, Rumpelstiltskin-like, it is nigh impossible to guess a cat's *real* name. Perhaps we should follow the advice of the ancient Chinese saying that to know what a cat is thinking you must hold its paw in your hand for a long time. However, for those with less patience it is hoped that the following lexical anthology will be of some help.

Naming anything, but especially cats, says as much about the giver as the receiver. Mark Twain apparently deliberately christened his cats with titles such as Appollinaris, Blatherskite and Zoroaster so that his children could practise pronouncing difficult words, whilst Beverley Nichols gave up altogether and simply numbered his. A well-known spoonerism has given rise to a plethora of cats called Cooking Fat, and a newspaper small ad once described a lost kitten as answering to the name of 'Go Away'... People can be unkind. They can also show a surprising lack of foresight — unlike human terms of endearment, pet names are public property, something to bear in mind for cats that need calling in at night or have to be rescued from trees by grinning neighbours and firemen. It is important, too, to heed Ogden Nash's words: 'The trouble with a kitten is/THAT/Eventually it becomes a/CAT'. Little Fluffikins of yesteryear is likely to resent his childhood title when he becomes the local bruiser.

In Lewis Carroll's *Through The Looking Glass*, Humpty Dumpty's complaint that Alice's name, unlike his, has no meaning is rather misleading. In fact most names — even proper names — have some logic (Alice derives from an old word for 'noble'). Some are based on colour and physical characteristics — such as Snowdrop (Alice's white kitten) or Algernon, meaning 'whiskered'. Others came from allusions, puns and other kinds of wordplay, like Oliver the cat that always asks for more, Pizza for a mongrel that is pizza this and pizza that, Wellington for one that has boots, and so on.

Aldous Huxley once said 'If you want to write, keep cats' and, not surprisingly perhaps, it is the wordsmiths who have given their cats the most fascinating names, many of which I have included in this analogy. However, not everyone has the ability with language that writers possess and finding an appropriate monicker for your moggie can be a nightmare, especially if confronted with a newly acquired adult that is perfectly aware of what they think is a suitable inscription for their identity disc — and will respond to no other.

Thus as well as lists of names based on fur- and eye-colour and pattern, this book also includes sections on feline fables, facts and feats that might help sparks of intuition to ignite in the reader's mind and generate that perfect name that you feel is right for your cat. Tales from myth, legend, religion and sorcery are followed by descriptions of famous owners and cats in the arts. Then come accounts of fictional felines, anecdotes about cats celebrated in their own right, TV and cinema stars, and some rather unusual varieties. Finally there are reports of record-breaking cats, cats in cartoons, a miscellany of oddball folklore and curios and, by way of a tailpiece, some suggestions for naming groups of cats.

Cat names which occur in the text are highlighted in bold type and those suggested by association appear at the end of each entry in brackets. In all, more than 2,000 names are given. But this book is by no means a definitive collection — there are plenty of reference works available in public libraries to satisfy the curiosity of the student of nomenclature. Rather, it is aimed at those who need a spur to get their minds into gear, a *catalyst* to start a train of thought. After all, only you can christen your cat. But it is hoped that this little compendium of names might prove of some assistance in the quest to discover one suitable for your pet. And if cats could talk, well I am sure there would be plenty more...

BLACKS AND BLACK-AND-WHITES

Adolf — After Adolf the Air Force cat (see *Record-Breaking Cats*).

Angus — For a beefy Scottish cat, after the famous Aberdeen Angus cattle.

Asbolos — From the Greek meaning 'soot-coloured' (one of Actaeon's hounds).

Ashanti — A noble warrior tribe from Ghana.

Bagheera — After the boy-cub Mowgli's protector in Kipling's *The Jungle Book*. Bagheera was the black panther who watched over Mowgli as he grew up amongst the wolves and kept the evil **Shere Khan**, the lame tiger, from killing him. (*Mowgli*)

Belisha — For a black-and-white striped cat with a red nose?

Benedict — Benedictine monks wear black.

Blackberry/Blackcurrant/Blackthorn — For fruity or prickly cats.

Blackguard — A dastardly cad, a bounder.

Blackie — After Britain's most affluent cat (see *Record-Breaking Cats*).

Blackjack — Another name for the ace of spades. Also a dark

mineral, a tar-covered leather mug, a black-barked oak tree, an American truncheon or a game of cards...the choice is yours. Black Jack was also a famous cat at the British Museum (see *Twins and Multiples*).

Bowler — For a City-slicker type with a smooth felt coat.

Bryony — Black bryony has greenish flowers and red berries, so for a black cat with green or red eyes.

Bustopher Jones — The fat black cat with white spats in T.S. Eliot's *Old Possum's Book of Practical Cats*. (**Eliot**)

Buttons — After the record-breaking eight-year-old female of this name (see *A Cat Miscellany*).

Caliban — The witch Sycorax's dark and monstrous son in Shakespeare's *The Tempest*. (**Shakespeare, Sycorax**)

Caruso — After a black cat with green eyes owned by the writer and critic Edmund Gosse (1849-1928). And perhaps also for a neutered male that sings a lot? (**Edmund**)

Charcoal — For a carbon-coloured or very dark grey puss.

Checkers/Chess — A black-and-white cat (Richard Nixon had a cocker spaniel called Checkers).

Chesterton — A black cat with a white bib and paws owned and painted by cat artist Lesley Anne Ivory.

Chiaroscuro — For a black-and-white cat or one with a combination of light and shade in its coat.

Cimmerian — A people who lived in the land of darkness in Greek myth and hence a word meaning 'very dark'.

Cleopatra — A beautiful dark Egyptian queen (see *Twins and Multiples*).

Columbine — After Thomas Carlyle's cat (see *Cats of the Famous*). Also for a white or grey cat (*columba* is Latin for 'dove'). (**Carlyle**)

Courageous — A Superman-like cat hero created by Bob Kane for TV. Black-and-white with green eyes and dressed in a red tunic with a gold-star motif and yellow cape, Courageous Cat and his sidekick Minute Mouse fight evil everywhere, especially when perpetrated by the sinister character known as The Frog. For a heroic cat.

Dexter — After the all-black Irish cattle (in fact cats are left-handed or south-paw so perhaps **Sinister** might be a better name for a particularly evil one).

Dirty Dick — The greatest Black Persian cat of all time. Born in 1911 he won no less than fourteen championships.

Domino — For a black cat with white spots or a white cat with black spots.

Doodlebug — For a black bombshell with a yellow-tipped tail?

Dougal — A Celtic name meaning 'black stranger'.

Duana — Gaelic for 'little dark girl'.

Dubbin — A well-known blacking for football boots — for a sporty cat or one who likes playing with balls?

Duffy — From the Irish Gaelic meaning 'dark-complexioned'.

Ebony — A warm black colour for a warm black cat.

Edward — After the Black Prince (1330-76), son of Edward III and victor of the battles of Crécy and Poitiers. For a pugnacious puss.

Felix — After Felix the black-and-white cartoon cat (see *Comical Cats*).

Geordie — An old name for a coalminer.

Guinness — For an all-black cat with a white collar, head or tip to its tail. Particularly for a stout cat!

Hecate — Greek goddess of the Underworld and goddess of witches — a good name for a black cat.

Humbug — For a black-and-white (or brown-and-white) cat, after the striped peppermint sweet.

Inky/Inkspot/Blotters — A Permanent Black cat.

Jack — (See 'Blackjack'.)

James — For a squat, penguin-like black-and-white tom, after TV's James the Cat who has had 'Fame, money and all that' and is now getting fat. Left behind when his owners moved

house he now lives in the garden with stray animal friends including Rocky the Rabbit and Freda the Kangaroo, and tends to brag a lot.

Jellicle — 'Jellicle cats are black and white' according to Eliot's poem.

Jet — For a fast black cat that is a gem.

Juniper — After the black berries from this plant. Also perhaps Jennifer for a female, from Donovan's song 'Jennifer Juniper'. (***Donovan***)

Kala — The Hindi word for 'black' and after some of the first Himalayan cats bred in the UK in the 1930s: Kala **Dawn**, Kala **Sabu** etc.

Kieran — A Celtic name meaning 'black'.

Korky — Star of the long-running cover-cartoon of D.C. Thomson's *Dandy* comic, Korky the Cat is remarkably human. He talks, walks on two legs and gets into all kinds of scrapes. A black cat with white paws, face and bib, a white tip to his tail and a red nose.

Krazy Kat — George Herriman's immortal comic-strip cat appeared in five separate animated film series between 1916 and 1963 and the character, together with companions Ignatz Mouse and Offisa Bull Pupp the dog, is now a cult classic. For a crazy cat. (***Herriman, Ignatz***)

Leila/Layla — An Arabic name meaning 'dark as night' and also the name of a heroine of ancient Persian legend — not to mention the title of Eric Clapton's famous rock song. For a cat to write home about. (***Clapton***)

Licorice/Liquorice — After the black sweet made from the root of this plant.

Lilith — Lilith was Adam's first wife, according to Rabbinical literature, who fled him and became a demon. It was also the name given to the poet Mallarmé's much-loved black cat which was sketched by Whistler (see also *A Cat Miscellany*). (***Mallarmé, Whistler***)

Lillian — Lillian was the black cat in Damon Runyon's story that had had her milk laced with Scotch since she was a kitten (see *Fictional Cats*) — so for a hardbitten cat. (Lillian means 'lily flower' so it is also a good name for a white cat.) (**Damon**)

Lucifer — One of Cardinal Richelieu's many cats (see *Cats of the Famous*) and one in Walt Disney's *Cinderella*. For a truly villainous creature. (**Richelieu, Walt**)

Lucky — Black cats are often said to be lucky, especially if they cross your path, but the real 'good luck' cat is the very rare Korat from Thailand.

Magic — For a black-magic cat or one who loves chocolates?

Magpie — A black-and-white cat with a thieving habit.

Mamelouk — Mamelouk is the big, black cat in the animated feature based on Margery Sharp's book, *The Rescuers*, and lives with the jailer in the Black Castle. The refined Miss Bianca mouse saves her mice companions and the Norwegian poet they have come to rescue by arguing with Mamelouk, thus distracting him so he loosens his grip. For a large, evil, half-Persian cat. (**Margery**)

Maria — After the Black Maria police van — for a cat that always breaks the rules.

Max — (See *Exotics and Rare Breeds*.)

Melanie — A name deriving from the Greek *melas* ('black').

Merle — Another name for the blackbird and also indicating a bluish-grey coat with black streaks so perhaps also for a tabby.

Midnight — The blackest cat of them all.

Minet — After a famous Post Office kitten (see *A Cat Miscellany*).

Minnaloushe — The dancing cat in Yeats's famous poem 'The Cat and the Moon' (see *Fictional Cats*). (**Yeats**)

Mistoffelees — After Eliot's 'Original Conjuring Cat'.

Mole/Metro — For a black cat that loves burrowing under clothes, into bags etc. or just adores digging up the garden!

Mr Toby — After Andrew Lang's cat. Toby was also the name of Mr Punch's dog. (**Andrew**)

Mysouff — After Alexandre Dumas's telepathic cat (see *Top Cats*). (**Alexandre**)

Natalie — Natalie is the name of the black cat that appears in the Giles cartoons (named after writer Nat Gubbins).

Nelson — After a large black cat owned by Winston Churchill (see *Cats of the Famous*). (**Winston**)

Nigel — From the Latin word *niger* meaning 'black'.

Nocturne — A sophisticated cat not averse to a little night music.

Odile — The Black Swan in *Swan Lake*.

Othello — After Shakespeare's 'Moor of Venice'.

Padre — A good name for a black cat with a white dog-collar. (Sir Roy Strong owned a cat called the **Reverend Wenceslas Muff** painted by Martin Leman — see also Rev. Dr John Langbourne in *Cats of the Famous*.) (**Roy**)

Panda — After a black-and-white kitten rescued by the PDSA-medal-winning Faith of St Paul's in World War II (see *Top Cats*).

Pekan — A kind of North American marten also known as a 'blackcat'.

Penguin — For a black-and-white cat that likes being

p-p-picked up!

Peta — (See *Exotics and Rare Breeds.*)

Peter — After the black-and-white cat that turned Louis Wain into a cat artist (see *Cats in the Arts*) and a black cat once employed at London's Savoy Hotel (see *A Cat Miscellany*). (**Louis**)

Piebald/Skewbald — For a black-and-white type.

Pluto — The Greek god of the Underworld and the tormented one-eyed cat in Edgar Allan Poe's grisly tale (see *Fictional Cats*).

Pontoon — Another name for the card game 'blackjack'.

Prince — After the Black Prince (see 'Edward').

Prudence — After French statesman Georges Clemenceau's cat (see *Cats of the Famous*). (**Clemenceau**)

Puffin — After the black-and-white bird.

Rameses — After any one of the 12 kings who ruled Egypt from the 14th to the 11th century BC.

Rasselas — Prince of Abyssinia in Dr Johnson's romance of the same name.

Rutterkin — After the malevolent familiar of Joan Flower (see *Legendary Cats*). (**Flower**)

Satchmo — For a very noisy, constantly yowling male black cat, after Louis 'Satchmo' ('big-mouth') Armstrong. (**Armstrong**)

Sexton — A gravedigger, so perhaps for a churchyard cat.

Simon — After the heroic black-and-white neutered tom of the Yangtse Incident (see *Top Cats*).

Simone — Simone Simon is the beautiful woman who turns into a panther in the 1942 thriller *Cat People*.

Sixby — 6B is a very black pencil.

Snoopy — For a curious black-and-white cat that thinks it's a dog?

Spider — A cat that climbs well, catches flies and seems to be all legs?

Spooky — For a wicked black cat, or alternatively, for a white, ghost-like feline. Spooky was also a cat that appeared in comic strips in the USA.

Stoker/Sweep — For coal-black cats.

Sylvester — After the Warner Brothers' scrawny black-and-white lisping cartoon cat (see *Comical Cats*).

Tadpole — For a small, glossy black cat with a long tail and a big head.

Taki — Raymond Chandler's black Persian. (*Raymond*)

Teach — Blackbeard the pirate's real name was Edward Teach — for a piratical puss. (*Blackbeard*)

Tom — A round-the-world black-and-white male (see *Record-Breaking Cats*).

Topper — After the hat, for a silky, rather formal cat.

Voodoo — (See *Exotics and Rare Breeds*.)

Zoë — This is the Greek word meaning 'life' and thus a very appropriate appellation for a lively cat. It was also the name of a black-and-white cat owned by Dante Gabriel Rossetti, painter and poet. And after Zoë Stokes, painter and owner of many cats. (*Dante*)

Zorilla — A black-and-white skunk-like creature.

Zorro — After the TV masked swordsman, dressed in black, who always leaves his mark — for a cat that does likewise! (*Zorro* is Spanish for 'fox', so perhaps also for a foxy feline.)

LEGENDARY
CATS

Cats in the Ark

According to some legends there weren't any cats in the Ark with Noah, and indeed none are mentioned in the Bible. However, one story has it that Noah and his family were so afraid of the lion that the great patriarch prayed to God for help and God gave the lion a fever which quietened him down considerably. The mice also became a problem and there was concern lest they should eat all their provisions and clothes. Once again Noah knelt down to the Almighty and in reply the lion suddenly sneezed. As he did so a cat sprang out from his nostrils, which so frightened the mice that they hid in holes and have done ever since.

A similar story about the origin of the cat is the legend of St Francis de Paola. Having tried everything in his power to distract the devout hermit from his prayers, as a last resort Satan sent hundreds of mice into his cell, which nibbled at his feet and clothes and caused him great torment. None the less, the holy man kept praying and suddenly a small furry animal rushed out of the sleeve of his habit and rapidly killed all the mice. However, two of the rodents managed to escape by hiding in a crack in the wall, which is why cats sit motionless in front of every nook and cranny to this day — waiting and watching to find the two that got away... (**Noah**, *Francis*, *Sneezer*, *Sleeves*)

The legend of Galanthis

In Ovid's *Metamorphoses* the legend is told of how **Galanthis** assisted in the birth of the great classical hero, Hercules. Alcmena, the wife of Amphitryon, king of Thebes, was made pregnant by Zeus in the guise of her husband and lay in considerable pain with the birth. Convinced that Zeus's wife and goddess of childbirth, Juno, had deliberately cast a spell on her mistress, Alcmena's servant Galanthis decided to play a trick to free the child. Approaching Juno, Galanthis broke the jealous goddess's concentration by announcing that Hercules had been born and that she should come and congratulate the mother. By thus distracting her the charm was broken, the boy was indeed born and Galanthis laughed at the success of her ruse. However, Juno was so incensed that she grabbed Galanthis's red hair and dragged her down to the ground, transforming her into a ginger cat for ever. (*Ovid, Juno, Zeus*)

Shippeitaro and the monster cat

A well-known Japanese legend tells the story of a wandering knight who, travelling through the mountains, came across a ruined temple and, as darkness fell, decided to sleep there. However, as midnight approached he was awoken by a band of dancing cats, who, oblivious of his presence, all shouted loudly 'Tell it not to Shippeitaro!' and then vanished. The following day he arrived at a village where everyone seemed to be greatly agitated and on enquiry he learnt that this was the day that the villagers had to pay their annual tribute to the evil cat-monster of the mountain. Every year they had to sacrifice their fairest maiden to the beast who would drag her to its lair in the ruined temple and then devour her. Recalling his experiences of the previous night the warrior asked who Shippeitaro was and learnt that it was a big brave dog belonging to the Prince's headman. At this the knight asked for the dog to be

sought out and put in the cage instead of the maiden and together with some villagers he carried it up the mountain to the ruined temple, When midnight struck the phantom cats again appeared in the temple but this time they were accompanied by an enormous tom who paced round the cage. Then, before he could suspect a trick, the knight released Shippeitaro who grabbed the monster with his teeth whilst the knight slayed it with his sword. The other cats ran away in panic and the knight returned to the village a hero and everyone lived in peace thereafter. (*Shippeitaro*)

Sinh, or how the Birman got its coat

Legend has it that long ago in ancient Burma there was a beautiful white cat with yellow eyes called **Sinh**, who was one of a hundred sacred cats that were guardians of the temple of a golden, blue-eyed goddess known as Tsun-Kyan-Kse. Every day the chief priest of the temple, Mun-Ha, would sit before the statue of the goddess in deep contemplation and every day his faithful cat Sinh would worship at his side.

For many years the tranquillity of this holy routine continued until one sad day the temple was besieged by enemies and Mun-Ha was mortally wounded. As his master lay dying, still praying to the goddess, the noble Sinh climbed up on to Mun-Ha's shoulders and stared intently at the golden statue. In a flash his yellow eyes turned the deep blue of Tsun-Kyan-Kse's, his pure white fur was tinged with gold and his face, tail and legs became a dark earthy brown — except for his four paws which, having touched his blessed master's broken body, remained perfectly white.

Inspired by the sight of this extraordinary transformation, the other priests rallied and eventually drove the raiders out of the temple. Seven days later, having refused all food and drink after his master's death, the faithful Sinh died, still gazing at the golden goddess. Saddened at the death of their chief priest and

his noble cat, the other priests convened to decide who should succeed Mun-Ha, but before any discussion could begin an extraordinary event took place. In a single body all the remaining cats of the temple — each one now transformed into the colouring of the dead Sinh — crowded into the holy chamber and surrounded one of the priests. This was interpreted as a sign from Tsun-Kyan-Kse herself and the priest was duly elected their leader.

And to this day, all descendants of the sacred Birman cat have the remarkable colouring of their distinguished ancestor, Sinh. (*Tsun*, *Kyan*, *Mun-Ha*)

Good King Howel

Howel the Good was King of Wales in the 10th century and amongst the celebrated laws passed during his peaceful reign was one specifically concerned with the feline security guard at the royal granaries. Such was the importance of this noble beast in protecting the food supply from marauding mice and rats that it was decreed that anyone who stole or killed the royal cat would forfeit a ewe together with its fleece and lambs. Alternatively, the culprit's fine would be as much good-quality wheat as would, when piled up in a heap, entirely cover the cat if held upright by the tail with its nose touching the ground. Not quite its weight in gold as some cat-lovers might insist, but a sizeable fee in those days none the less — though presumably Manx and Japanese bobtail cats were not much in favour amongst Welsh princes at that time...(*Howel*)

Dick Whittington and his cat

There have been hundreds of mayors of London since the post was first created in 1191 but the names of all but one have disappeared into obscurity — no doubt this is entirely due to their lack of interest in cats!

Richard Whittington was born about 1359 the son of

Sir Richard Whittington of Gloucestershire and, being the youngest of five sons, didn't inherit any of the family wealth when his father died and was completely orphaned when his mother also died when he was 13. Hearing that the streets of London were paved with gold, he set off to make his fortune and by chance managed to find a job working in the kitchens of a rich City merchant. However, the cook was unkind to him and his garret room was infested with rats and mice so when a visitor gave him a penny he spent it all on a cat.

One day the merchant was fitting out a cargo ship for a trading mission overseas and, as was then the custom, invited the staff to participate in the venture and take a share of the profits. Having nothing else to donate, Dick reluctantly offered his cat, which was taken on board. However, no sooner had the ship set sail than the cook began to abuse him again and, without the comfort of his cat, Dick decided to run away. He had reached the hill leading up to the outlying village of Highgate when the pealing of the mighty bells of Bow church seemed to ring out 'Turn again Whittington, Lord Mayor of London' and he returned to the merchant's house and the cook's scolding.

Meanwhile, the cargo ship had reached the Barbary Coast which was overrun with rats and when the captain lent the king Dick's cat to clear out his palace, the king was so pleased that he gave them a casket of jewels. On their return to England the jewels were presented to Dick as his share from the trip and he became the richest commoner in the country. He then married the merchant's daughter, became master mercer, alderman, sheriff and then mayor in quick succession and was a close favourite of King Henry IV. Never was a penny so well spent! (**Whittington**, **Mayor**, **Barbary**, **Highgate**)

Gunduple and the golden mouse

There is an old legend from Borneo that tells the story of a lame boy whose daily duty it was to see that all the young children in the village got safely to and from school without being attacked by wild animals or eaten by goblins. However, one day an evil goblin called Pasangu waylaid the group in the form of a crying child and when some of them came over to comfort him he led them off into the forest, never to be seen again. The villagers were very angry when they heard this and threatened to throw the lame boy and his pet cat **Gunduple** out of the village altogether. But the boy complained that he was not being sufficiently rewarded for his services and, demanding a cottage of his own and some land, promised to rid the village of the goblin once and for all. The villagers reluctantly agreed and the very next day the boy summoned all the children and warned them not to trust anything in the forest except for mice, telling them that the only form the goblin was unable to take was a mouse. Now the goblin got to hear of this and, hoping to capture all the children at once, turned himself into a golden mouse with bells around its neck and a long bright tail. However, when the golden mouse appeared and the children started chasing after it, the cunning boy released his trusty cat Gunduple, who quickly caught the dazzling creature and gobbled up goblin and mouse in one. (***Borneo, Goblin, Pasangu***)

King of the Cats

The following story has appeared in many guises over the years, famous examples being the versions told by Sir Walter Scott to Washington Irving and by 'Monk' Lewis to Shelley. But in all variants the basic framework is the same. Late at night a traveller passes a ruined abbey and sees a procession of cats carrying a small coffin with a crown on it which they lower into a grave. Horrified by the apparition, the traveller hastens from

the spot and when he reaches his destination he tells a friend what he has seen. But scarcely has he finished when his friend's cat, sleeping tranquilly by the fireside when he came in, suddenly springs up, cries out 'Then I am the King of the Cats!' and disappears up the chimney. (*Walter*, *Scott*, *Lewis*, *Rex*)

Freya and her felines

The ancient Scandinavian goddess Freya was greatly revered in olden times — to such an extent that she had a day of the week named after her: Freytag or Friday. As, like Venus, she was identified as the goddess of love and beauty, Friday used to be regarded as the most appropriate day on which to marry, and this was only changed in the Northern Hemisphere when Christianity took root and it was deemed unsuitable to wed on the day of Jesus's death. Blue-eyed and golden-haired, Freya rode a heavenly chariot drawn by two cats which reflected her own dual role, for not only are cats one of the most loving and affectionate of domestic animals, but they can also be extremely fierce — as Freya was when she led the Valkyrie into battle.

An ancient Scandinavian farmers' ritual involved putting a pan of milk in the cornfields for Freya's cats to drink as they passed by and in return she would protect their crops. (*Freya*, *Freytag*, *Friday*, *Valkyrie*)

Bast, the cat goddess

Bast, who is sometimes identified with the Roman goddess Diana (Greek Artemis), was a companion of the sun god Ra and a major deity in ancient Egypt. She is usually represented with a cat's or lion's head and a human body, and a number of black basalt statues of her have been found at Thebes and elsewhere. Herodotus described Bast's shrine at Bubastis ('city of Bast'), east of the Nile delta, as being made of red granite, 500 feet long, 60 feet high and surrounded by a moat 100 feet wide. Over

700,000 people would attend the annual festival held there every April and May and a great deal of wine would be consumed in the goddess's honour.

As is well known, cats were much revered throughout ancient Egypt but particularly in cities dedicated to Bast, such as Bubastis and Speos Artemidos ('cave of Artemis'), and if cats died they would be embalmed and sent from all over the country for burial at such centres. Also, if a feline death occurred in the family then all its members should shave their eyebrows. This practice doesn't seem to have carried through to the present century but Bast is still very much amongst us, for, according to some scholars, our modern form of addressing our pets as 'puss' derives from 'pasht', a variant of the goddess's name. (**Bubastis**, **Ra**, *Speos*, **Pasht**)

Patripatan, the celestial cat

Long ago in ancient India there were two holy men — a Brahmin and a Penitent — who were constantly bickering over which of them was the most virtuous. The court of King Salingham and the king himself could not decide between the two, such were the number of challenges they gave each other.

One day the Brahmin declared that he was so virtuous that he was able to enter any of the Seven Heavens and the Penitent — knowing that his rival had overstepped himself as no mortals are allowed there — accepted the challenge and asked the Brahmin to pick a flower from the unique Parisadam tree that only grows in the heaven of Devendiren and bring it back to the court. Confident that at last he would be declared the winner the Penitent watched the Brahmin depart, only to be amazed when he later reappeared carrying the requested bloom. However, refusing to acknowledge defeat, the Penitent then declared that he was so holy that even his cat **Patripatan** would be honoured in Devendiren. The cat was duly sum-

31

moned and disappeared into the clouds. However, when it didn't return all became anxious, but what had happened was that one of the goddesses had fallen in love with the beautiful cat and wouldn't let it return to earth. Eventually, after 300 years, the cat appeared in a blaze of glory in the sky, seated in majesty on a magnificent throne, and presented the king with a complete branch of flowers from the Parisadam tree. Despite cries of 'Victory' the Brahmin refused to accept defeat, claiming that the cat deserved half the credit, and the matter was never finally resolved. However, the cat itself became the chief ornament of the court and was universally praised and admired and every day would dine with the king and sit on his shoulder. (*Salingham, Parisadam, Devendiren, Brahmin*)

Blockula and the satanic cats

The first witchcraft trial in England was held in 1566 during the reign of Elizabeth I when Agnes Waterhouse and her daughter Joan — owners of a white-spotted cat called **Satan** — were executed. The last was conducted over a century later in 1684, but as evidence that witch hysteria was still powerful even at this late date, in 1669 an extraordinary trial took place in the Swedish village of Motira. Over 300 children aged between six and 16 confessed to all kinds of unimaginable evils and admitted to being in league with the Devil. As well as directing their supposed misdeeds, Satan himself had apparently given each a 'carrier' in the form of a young cat who helped them steal butter, cheese, milk and bacon which they would carry to his palace, Blockula, as offerings. The lunacy of the bewitched children was, however, surpassed by the judges who sent 15 of them to the gallows and 36 more were condemned to be whipped in front of the church door every Sunday for a year. (*Agnes, Joan, Motira, Blockula*)

The white cat

Long ago there was an old king who knew that he would soon have to abdicate in favour of one of his three sons. But though they pressed him he didn't feel ready to give up his power and sent them off to travel the world for a year — whoever brought back the most beautiful dog would be king. The princes went off on their separate ways and after a time the youngest came to a magnificent castle which appeared to be uninhabited. However, as he stepped inside, disembodied hands took his coat, brushed his hair, waited on him at supper and escorted him to his bedroom. The following day they led him to a beautiful white cat seated on a throne in a splendid hall, who greeted him warmly and took him hunting mounted on a monkey, chasing squirrels with a pack of cats. As the year passed the white cat and the prince grew fond of each other but the young man knew he had to return and he still hadn't found a dog. So the cat gave him a casket which she told him to open in front of the king and all would be well. The prince returned to his father's kingdom and, though his brothers had found rare and exotic dogs, when he opened the casket an exquisite tiny dog sprang out of a walnut shell and he was declared the winner.

However, the king still demurred and sent his sons off again to find a piece of cambric fine enough to pass through the eye of a needle. Again the youngest spent the year with the cat and again she gave him a casket. This time the prince's brothers' pieces of cambric were very fine but wouldn't pass through the king's needle. But when the prince opened his casket he found a walnut shell, inside which was a nutshell, then a cherry stone, then a grain of wheat, then a grain of millet and inside the millet was a piece of cambric 400 yards long which easily fitted the needle.

Still the king was not satisfied and sent the princes off again to find the most beautiful woman they could. The youngest

returned to the white cat who told him to cut off her head and tail and all would be well. With great sadness he did so and the cat changed into a beautiful princess. Having explained that he had thereby released her from the spell of a wicked fairy, the princess accompanied the prince to court where she was by far the most beautiful woman and the king gave his youngest son the kingdom. However, as the princess already had four kingdoms herself, she gave one each to the other two brothers, married the prince and together they ruled over the rest.

Rutterkin, a sinful cat

Another satanic cat from the early 17th century was the 'familiar' of Joan Flower — a sinister, malevolent black creature 'with eyne of burning coal'. The story is told in the *Church Boke of Bottesford* that Joan so hated the Earl of Rutland and his noble wife that she stole one of the gloves of their eldest son, Henry, soaked it in water, pricked it with pins and rubbed it across the evil **Rutterkin**'s back. Shortly afterwards Henry died. The procedure was repeated with a glove from the younger son and he too died. As a finale, feathers were stolen from the countess's bed and rubbed over Rutterkin's belly to prevent her having any more children.

All these details were given in evidence by Joan Flower's daughters, Margaret and Phyllis — who had stolen the gloves and feathers — and were stoutly denied by their mother, to no avail. However, she continued to protest her innocence to the last and when in prison prayed that the bread she was eating would choke her to death if she was guilty of sorcery — it did! Her wicked children were hanged in 1618 but there is no record of what became of the cat... (**Flower, Bottesford, Margaret, Phyllis**)

Why the cat's back is curved

A Finnish legend has it that when Jumala the Creator had made Man he showed him to the Devil who responded by creating a mouse saying, 'I have made a jumper'. Jumala then said he would make a wrestler and created a cat which he threw at the mouse, which ran away in terror. The Devil was so angered by this that he grabbed the cat by its head and tail and bent it nearly double and it has remained so ever since. (*Jumala*)

Serpent-slaying cats

Apart from the mongoose, the cat is the only animal that is not afraid of snakes. It is also remarkably skilful at despatching them, another reason why the cat was so venerated in Egypt where snakes abound and no doubt the inspiration for its association with the sun-god **Ra** who is often depicted in the form of a cat destroying the evil snake-god of darkness, Apep.

A more recent legend of snakicide by cats is narrated by the 18th-century French writer Moncrif. Apparently a promontory in Cyprus used to be known as the Cape of Cats, after the large number of the creatures that could once be seen there. They had belonged to a monastery that had formerly stood on the cape and had been kept by the monks to destroy the hordes of poisonous black-and-white snakes that infested the area. Every day they would be released to roam at will amongst the serpent population but, snake snacks notwithstanding, they would always return to the monastery when the meal-bell sounded. (*Apep*, *Moncrif*)

WHITES, CREAMS
AND GOLDS

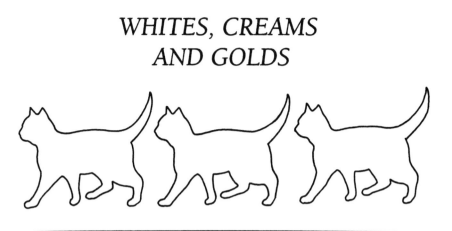

Ajax — After the Greek hero and the white scouring powder — a powerful puss.

Alabaster — A very fine-grained variety of gypsum used for statues — for a statuesque white cat.

Alban — Meaning 'white'.

Amarillo/Amaryllis/Belladonna — *Amarillo* is the Spanish word for 'yellow'. Also after the white-flowered plant *Amaryllis Belladonna*. (*Belladonna* means 'beautiful lady' in Italian — another good name.)

Aneurin — A name meaning 'truly golden'.

Apricot — After the downy yellow fruit whose name itself means 'early ripening', so perhaps for a precocious puss.

Arthur — The first really big feline TV star — the Kattomeat King (see *Screen Cats*).

Ashley — For an ash-blonde cat.

Asphodel — A yellow flower which reputedly covered the Elysian Fields in Greek mythology.

Aubrey — From the Teutonic for 'blond ruler'.

Bamboo/Bamboozle — For a golden-yellow cat that just loves confusion?

Banquo — The ghost that haunts Macbeth in Shakespeare's play. (*Macbeth*)

Barley — A creamy-white cat, or for a precious puss that's always in a stew (pearl barley)?

Béchamel — For a saucy cat.

Belo/Bianca/Blanka/Blondie — Various names meaning 'white'.

Blossom — For a perfect flower of a cat.

Bourbon — After the white flag of the French Bourbon kings, or perhaps for a brown, after the biscuit.

Boyd — The Celtic name meaning 'yellow'.

Bridie — A wedding-white type.

Brimstone — The original 'butter-coloured fly' from which the species gets its name; also an old name for sulphur and for a scolding nagging woman.

Bronwen — Welsh for 'white bosom'.

Bull's-eye — After the striped peppermint sweet (yellow/white and black).

Cambric — A fine white linen cloth.

Camembert — After the creamy French cheese.

Candide/Candida/Candesse — Meaning 'brilliant white'.

Candy — A white flossy type.

Carambola — A yellow, smooth-skinned edible fruit.

Carmel — The Carmelites are also known as White Friars.

Carnation — 'All the family love Carnation', as the advertisement for this brand of evaporated milk used to run. A popular cat like a pretty flower?

Chalky — For a Foreign White or any other chalk-coloured variety, or even, by contrast, for a jet-black cat with a sense of humour.

Chanterelle — Yellow-gold edible funnel-shaped mushrooms, from the Latin for a drinking vessel so perhaps also for a cat that drinks (or sings — French *chanter*) a lot.

Charlie Chan — After the wealthiest cat in the world (see *Record-Breaking Cats*).

Charollais — Large French cream-coloured beef cattle.

Chartreuse — For a yellow cat, or one with yellow or green eyes.

Chips — Fish is never very far from Chips...

Clover/Alsike/Melilot — After the white varieties of this plant (alfileria or 'pin clover' is pink or purple, for a cat with points of these colours).

Colorado — For a yellow cat with longitudinal black stripes — after the potato-blight beetle.

Crystal — After the classic pedigree female Persian White owned by the Hon. Mrs McLaren Morrison, and also after the Crystal Palace in London where the first cat shows were held. (*Morrison*)

Cupid — (See *Exotics and Rare Breeds*.)

Custard — After the egg and milk sweet.

Cymbeline — A Celtic name meaning 'lord of the sun'.

Cyrus — (See *Exotics and Rare Breeds*.)

Daffodil/Dilly — After the yellow narcissus, national emblem of Wales (so also for a Cymric cat?). **Narcissus** would also be a good name for a self-regarding puss.

Daisy — For a white cat with a yellow face.

Daz — A dazzlingly white cat, perhaps speckled with blue like the washing-powder.

Dominic — For a white cat with a black head, after the Dominican monks who wear white habits with black hoods.

Dorado — Spanish for 'golden'. *Eldorado* means 'the golden one'.

Elvira — From the Latin for 'blonde' and a ghost in Noël Coward's *Blithe Spirit*.

Ermine — The winter coat of the stoat is white with a black-tipped tail. The fur is also used for ceremonial dress,

so for a superior cat. (The word 'ermine' comes from *Armenius mus* meaning 'Armenian mouse'!) (*Noël*)

Fenella — A Celtic name meaning 'she of white shoulders'.

Fingal — From the Celtic meaning 'white stranger'.

Flavia/Fulvia — Two classic Roman names, meaning, respectively, 'yellow-' and 'tawny-coloured'. Fulvia was also the name of Mark Antony's wife, whom the catty Cleopatra refers to in Shakespeare's play as 'shrill-tongued Fulvia'. (*Mark*)

Flossy/Flosche — Silky white fibres from cotton are called 'floss', from the old French word *flosche* meaning 'down'.

Galatea — From the Greek word meaning 'milky white', for a cat of that colour. The sculptor Pygmalion made an ivory statue, called it Galatea and fell in love with it. In answer to his prayers the goddess Aphrodite breathed life into it and it became his wife, mother of Paphos. The legend was the basis for Shaw's play, *Pygmalion,* upon which the film *My Fair Lady* is based.

Gandhi — A white cat with brown legs and head?

Gardenia — After the fragrant, white-flowered shrub.

Genevieve — Celtic for 'white noble one'.

Gilda — Old English for 'golden'.

Gwendolyn — An old Welsh word meaning 'white-haired

one' and also the name of the wife of Merlin in the Arthurian legends. For a magical blonde cat.

Haldi — The Indian name for turmeric.

Havelock — After the white cloth worn at the back of French Legionnaires' hats.

Helio — From the Greek word meaning 'the sun'.

Hellmans — For a mayonnaise-coloured cat!

Hiver — French for 'winter', so for a white.

Honey/Honeybunch — For a sweet puss with a real buzz.

Honeysuckle — A pretty yellow type.

Igloo — For a frosty white cat.

Ivory — After cat painter Lesley Anne Ivory.

Jacob — A cream cracker of a cat! (Also after the painter Jacob Cats.)

Jasmine/Jessamine/Frangipani — After the yellow and white scented shrubs (frangipani sometimes has red flowers, for a darker coloured cat).

Jason — He of the Golden Fleece.

Javotte — A name meaning 'white stream'.

Jemimah — From the Hebrew word meaning 'a dove' (also for a grey cat).

Khaki — After the colour and for a cat that likes cars (car-key)?

Kittiwake — After the bird, for a white cat with black points or for a particularly wide-awake cat.

Klondyke — A gold-digging cat or a yellow tom in a rush.

Lillian — Means 'lily flower'.

Lily — Dr Johnson had a 'white kitling' called Lily.

Lux — Latin for 'light'.

Macaroni/Makaria — After the Italian yellow-white pasta or the Greek barley meal (*makaria*) but also after the 18th-century British dandies — for a foppish, affected cat.

Madonna/Marilyn — For sexy blondes.

Magnolia — A beautiful white.

Mango — A delicious sweet orange-yellow fruit.

Marcus — After **Coylum** Marcus, a famous US Champion White Persian.

Margaret/Maida/Megan — All from the Greek for 'a pearl'.

Marley — After the ghost in Dickens's *A Christmas Carol*.

Mazda — For the light of your life! (Also another name for Zoroaster, q.v.)

Miniver — Miniver is a white fur used in ceremonial costumes, so a good name for a white cat with a touch of class.

Minto — For a fresh white.

Moby-Dick — A great white whale of a cat, after the Herman Melville story.

Noodles — For a pasta-coloured puss or one lacking something upstairs?

Odette — The White Swan in *Swan Lake*.

Panama — A white cat with a black ring, after the hat.

Pangur Ban — The famous white cat in a 9th-century poem of that name written by an Irish monk at Reichenau (see *Fictional Cats*).

Peaches — A juicy, fruity, real peach of a cat.

Peanuts/Goober — 'Goober' is another name for a peanut. Also perhaps for a small-headed cat (and **KP** for a peanut-coloured one that's always in the kitchen?).

Pearl — For a precious white cat.

Percy — After the star of David Hockney's picture, *Mr and Mrs Clark and Percy*. (**David, Hockney**)

Persil — A whiter than white cat.

Pinchbeck — A zinc and copper alloy resembling gold.

Pineapple — A deceptively prickly customer.

Polo — After the white mint.

Popcorn — A white cat with lots of bounce.

Posset — After the curdled spicy hot milk drink.

Potto — A kind of lemur, particularly the golden variety.

Quartz — A sparkling white cat and also after Tom Quartz, President Roosevelt's cat (see *Top Cats*), itself named after one in a story by Mark Twain. (*Roosevelt*)

Quincy — A quince-coloured cat.

Rapunzel — The girl with the long golden hair in the Grimms' fairytale.

Roxanne — After the blonde astronomer in the Steve Martin film of the same name. For a star-gazing female.

Samantha — The real name of Arthur the Kattomeat TV star (see *Screen Cats*).

Satan — After an Elizabethan white-spotted cat owned by two alleged witches (see *Legendary Cats*), though black would seem to be a better colour.

Sepia — A pale brown cat, perhaps particularly for a photogenic one.

Sesame — After the yellow seed and for a cat good at opening doors?

Sherbet — A fizzy pussy.

Sherlock — Old English for 'fair' or 'white-haired' this would also be an appropriate name for any inquisitive cat — after Conan Doyle's sleuth, Sherlock Holmes. (*Conan*)

Snowball — After the cat caught in a tree in the film *Roxanne,* and Orwell's revolutionary pig in *Animal Farm*.

Snow White/Snowflake/Snowdrop — For incandescently white, purr-fect cats. (Snowdrop was also the white kitten in Lewis Carroll's *Through the Looking Glass*.)

Snowy — Not to be confused with Tintin's dog; for any white cat. Erasmus Darwin (1731-1808), poet, scientist and grandfather of Charles Darwin, owned a cat called Persian Snow. (*Tintin*, *Erasmus*, *Darwin*)

Solomon — From the Hebrew for 'peaceful' and also the real-life name of Bloefeld's long-haired cat in the Bond films (see *Screen Cats*). (*Bloefeld*)

Sorbet — A refreshing, frosty cat

Soriana — The ancient story of 'Puss in Boots' goes back a long way (see *Fictional Cats*) and in Straparola's Italian version the colour of the cat, who is called Soriana, is white. (*Straparola*)

Sponge — A yellow cat that drinks a lot of water!

Stilton — A white cat with blue points.

Sunflower — A beautiful sun-loving creature with a big head?

Sunshine — For a cat that puts all others in the shade.

Syllabub — A rich, sweet cat.

Tallow — A cat you can't hold a candle to! (Or one that gets on your wick?)

Toddy — After the milky-white alcoholic beverage — for a cat that keeps you warm at night.

Vanova — Meaning 'white wave'.

Whin — Another name for gorse, which has yellow flowers; for a prickly cat. (Wynn is another name meaning 'white'.)

White Heather — One of Queen Victoria's cats. (*Victoria*)

William/Williamina — Charles Dickens's white 'tom', renamed when it gave birth (see *Cats of the Famous*).

York/Yorkie — The white rose was the emblem of the House of York in the Wars of the Roses. Also perhaps for a tough, chocolate-coloured trucking cat?

Zora — The dawn.

Zoroaster — A Persian prophet and also the Persian word meaning 'golden star'.

CATS OF THE FAMOUS

Literary cats

The number of cats owned by literary figures is enormous and growing every day. Many are mentioned elsewhere in this book but perhaps a few more that are worthy of note are Thackeray's cat **Louisa**, Mark Twain's **Sour Mash**, Thoreau's companion **Min**, Victor Hugo's magnificent **Chanoine** that used to sit in splendour on a large red ottoman in the centre of the salon at his house in Paris, and Carlyle's black cat **Columbine**. Ernest Hemingway was also a great cat lover and had 30 of them when he was living in the Finca Vigia in Cuba. His explanation of why he owned so many was because of their 'absolute emotional honesty', and to show how much trust he had in them on one occasion he left his baby son in the sole charge of one called **F. Puss** when they lived in Paris.

Harriet Beecher Stowe of *Uncle Tom's Cabin* fame owned a large Maltese cat with a white underside called **Calvin** who just walked into her house one day, fully grown. When she moved to Florida she presented him to the writer Charles Dudley Warner who described his dignified deportment, intelligence and the fact that he never miaowed like other cats but merely uttered the occasional 'well-bred ejaculation'. When he died he was buried in a candle box beneath the hawthorn trees in the Warners' garden. (*Thackeray*, *Thoreau*, *Hugo*, *Carlyle*, *Hemingway*, *Harriet*, *Warner*)

Foss, a fussy pussy

It's not often that a cat has a house built especially for it, but the writer Edward Lear did exactly that. He was so fond of his stubby-tailed **Foss** — star of 'How Pleasant to Know Mr Lear' and 'The Heraldic Blazon of Foss the Cat', and undoubtedly the inspiration for 'The Owl and the Pussycat' — that when he moved house he had the new one in San Remo, Italy, built to exactly the same specifications as before just so that the cat would feel at home. (**Lear**)

Richelieu, the cat-loving cardinal

Louis XIII's chief minister, virtual dictator of France and one of the most powerful and feared statesmen of the 17th century, Armand Jean du Plessis — the iron-willed Cardinal Richelieu — was simply potty about cats. He may have crushed France's European rivals, the Habsburgs, and cruelly suppressed the Huguenots in his own country, but at home his 14 cats walked all over him — literally. Wherever he went in his palace in Paris at least a dozen cats would follow and two attendants were hired exclusively to look after their needs. He was particularly fond of kittens and his favourite cat was **Soumise**, who often slept on his lap. Others included **Gazette**, **Serpolet**, jet-black **Lucifer** and the rat-torturing **Ludovic the Cruel**.

Richelieu was also a considerable patron of the arts, wrote plays himself and even founded the prestigious Académie Française. So perhaps it is not surprising that he named two more of his cats after one of the members of this august assembly — **Racan** and **Perruque** were so-called because they were born in the academician's wig (*perruque*) which the absent-minded Racan had left lying about and their mother had adopted as a nest!

Richelieu's kindness to his cats even continued after his

death as each one of his pets — as well as their attendants — was left a sizeable pension in his will. (**Richelieu, Armand**)

A maternal cat

Jerome K. Jerome had a cat that was only happy if she had a family — 'Her brains had run entirely to motherliness, for she hadn't much sense.' The story goes that he once put an orphaned spaniel puppy amongst her kittens and she brought it up as her own. The poor puppy tried to miaow and wash its face with its paws but somehow never really got the hang of it and whenever it barked the cat would box its ears!

On another occasion they gave her a baby squirrel to rear. At first she was very proud of her new charge but couldn't seem to understand why its magnificent bushy tail kept sticking up over its head instead of lying flat like a normal cat's tail. No matter how many times she held it down with one paw and licked it to flatten it into shape, the tail just flicked back over the squirrel's head again. (**Jerome**)

Madame Théophile, a dainty cat

The French poet, novelist and critic Théophile Gautier had nine cats including **Childebrand, Eponine, Séraphita, Gavroche** and **Zizi** amongst others, but his favourite was **Madame Théophile** — a gorgeous red cat with a white breast and blue eyes, so named because of the intimacy of their relationship. Madame T. would follow Gautier everywhere, sleep on his bed, watch him write, eat at table with him, and was greatly adored by the author. She also loved perfumes and would go into ecstasies inhaling patchouli and vetiver. But though she was very fond of music and would sit on the piano whilst singers accompanied themselves, the high notes would make her nervous and if anyone happened to hit top A she would simply close the singer's mouth with her paw!

Another story relates how a friend of Gautier's asked him to

look after his huge green parrot for a few days. Never having seen such a creature before, Madame Théophile was at first intimidated by the strange animal, but after a while she plucked up courage and leapt up onto its perch only to be greeted by the parrot saying, in a deep bass voice: 'As tu déjeuné, Jacquot?' (Have you had your breakfast, Jack?') The terrified cat flew off the perch and disappeared under the bed for the rest of the day. The nightmare of the monstrous green chicken that talked held all further thoughts of assault in check until the owner returned to collect his remarkable bird later. (**Gautier, Jacquot**)

Vatican cats

No less than three popes are recorded as having had cats: Leo XII, Gregory XV and Pius IX. The latter's papal pussy would accompany him to his daily meals and sit obediently at table whilst the pontiff drank his soup. Once finished the Pope would then personally serve the cat its own bowl.

Leo XII's pet **Micetto** — a large grey-and-red cat banded with black — was born in the loggia of Raphael in the Vatican itself and would always sit on a fold of the Pope's white robe when he granted ambassadorial audiences etc. Accustomed to taking his daily promenade high up in the dome of St Angelo, Micetto was bequeathed to one of his most ardent admirers, the French writer/diplomat Chateaubriand, on Leo's death. (**Leo, Gregory, Pius, Chateaubriand**)

The sad case of Selima

If ever there was an instance of divine retribution or the biter bit it was that of the demise of the tabby **Selima**, adored pet of the 18th-century writer, Horace Walpole. Playing one day with some goldfish in her master's house at Strawberry Hill in London, she accidentally fell into the water and was drowned. But her memory lives on as her last moments were immortalized by the poet Thomas Gray in his 'Ode on the Death of

a Favourite Cat Drowned in a Tub of Gold Fishes' (1748).
(*Horace*, *Walpole*)

The Y cat

Ailurophiles as a race have ample opportunity to study the various positions cats assume when relaxing — and pretty extraordinary some of them are it will be agreed. But perhaps more unusual than most was the reposeful attitude regularly adopted by an old tabby female owned by the poet, painter and leader of the Pre-Raphaelite movement, D.G. Rossetti. After a hard day's lecturing at King's College, London, where he was at one time Professor of Italian, Rossetti would return home exhausted and collapse in front of the fire, quickly falling asleep flat out on the hearthrug. The cat, only temporarily disturbed by his arrival, would then take up her post beside him. Sitting upright on her haunches, she would stretch her forelegs out in the shape of a capital Y, hook the claws on the paws of her front feet into the crosswires of the fireguard and remain in this position warming herself until disturbed or supper called. Apparently her daughters failed to inherit the mannerism — evidently they never learnt the how and the wherefore of the Y!
(*Rossetti*, *Dante*, *Gabriel*)

Hinse, the dogfighting cat

Hinse of Hinsefield was Sir Walter Scott's pet cat, immortalized in a portrait of the great Scottish writer by Sir John Watson Gordon. However, what is not revealed from the demure expression of the cat as he sits quietly by a candle on his master's desk is that Hinse was the terror of the Scott household and ruled the family home — which included a number of dogs — with a rod of iron. Indeed, such was the power of the pugnacious old tom's steely paw that the writer's favourite hound — an enormous dog called Maida — would be reduced to a whimpering wreck whenever the cat blocked his passage. However, even a mighty

warrior like Hinse is only allowed nine lives, and he finally met his Waterloo when he took on Nimrod the bloodhound. Which just goes to prove that every dog has his day. (**Gordon**, **Maida**, **Nimrod**)

Lords of the lamp

Florence Nightingale, the Crimean War nurse known as 'the Lady of the Lamp', apparently at one time owned no less than 60 cats and her selfless devotion to the needs of the sick seems to have been passed on through generations of felines ever since. Mention is made elsewhere of Churchill's cat who warmed the statesman's feet when stricken low by flu and Poe's **Caterina** who comforted his dying wife. But an even greater act of nursing charity was recorded by the *Daily Sketch* in 1938, which reported the case of a cat donating blood to save its fellows in Denver, Colorado. **Buttercup**, a big yellow tom, had caught septicaemia, normally fatal to cats, and after a brief illness had recovered fully. Realizing that he must be immune, a vet then carried out a blood transfusion between Buttercup and two other cats suffering from the same disease, **Skeezix** and **Snicklefritz**, thereby saving their lives. An equally caring cat was **Fat Albert**, official blood donor of the Marlton Animal Hospital in New Jersey, USA, who regularly performed valorous acts to help sick cats from the early 1970s until his death in 1982. (**Florence**, **Nightingale**, **Churchill**, **Edgar**, **Denver**)

Britannia's cats

One of the earliest recorded legacies for cats was that made by 'La Belle Stewart' — Frances Theresa Stewart — whose will included pensions for her pets. Returning from exile in France in 1662 with the re-establishment of the monarchy under Charles II, she became Maid of Honour to Queen Catherine and was even rumoured to be the lover of the king himself. She was also

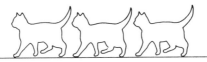

the model for the figure of Britannia on British copper coinage until decimalization. (*Britannia, Theresa, Catherine, Stewart*)

Dickensian cats

Charles Dickens was another celebrated lover of cats and always featured them in his writings, including no less than three in *Bleak House* alone — notably the savage **Lady Jane** who sat on Krook's shoulder. Dickens himself also owned a number of cats at his house in Gad's Hill. One of these, a white 'tom' called **William**, he was forced to rename **Williamina** when she had six kittens in his study. Despite constant efforts to clear the feline brood out of his work area, their mother persisted in bringing them back in until in desperation he managed to deposit the bulk of the litter with friends, keeping only one kitten — apparently born deaf — which he called **The Master's Cat**. However, the great author's peace of mind was short-lived, for the dear mite soon learnt a new trick all of her own — she would snuff out the candle Dickens was reading by with her paw! (*Dickens, Krook, The Master*)

A batty cat

The French novelist J. K. Huysmans was a well-known aliurophile and incorporated cats in many of his books. *En Rade* features his own grey cat, the philosophical but unattractive **Mouche**, who had green eyes, but the death scene is based on the real-life demise of his favourite tabby. This cat, called **Barre-en-Rouille**, was a big red-and-black-striped gutter cat that used to accompany Huysmans everywhere and would sit on his balcony at night catching bats like most cats do birds. (*Huysmans, Batty*)

Churchill's cats

Sir Winston Churchill had a number of cats over the years, one of which, a marmalade tom called **Tango**, was drawn by the

celebrated artist Sir William Nicholson who himself owned four. During the war years one of his ministers visited Churchill when he was laid up with flu at Chequers and entered his room to find the great statesman in bed with his large black cat **Nelson** purring contentedly on his feet. Seeing the minister's expression, Churchill announced, 'This cat does more for the war effort than you do. He acts as a hot-water bottle and saves fuel and power.' (**Nicholson, Chequers**)

Cats on a hot tin stove

Sir Compton Mackenzie, author of *Sinister Street* and *Whisky Galore* amongst others, was also a great cat lover — indeed he was for many years President of the Siamese Cat Club. Another celebrated ailurophile, Beverley Nichols, tells in his book, *Cats A-Z*, how he once visited Sir Compton on his remote island in the Hebrides and was amazed to discover four elderly Siamese cats sitting quietly on the kitchen range. After some coaxing he managed to get one of them to allow itself to be picked up and was surprised to feel the heat of its rear end which was considerably in excess of what a human could stand. Marvelling at the capacity of the creature to withstand such temperatures he carefully replaced the cat which, on being seated on the stove once more, began to purr happily 'like a kettle when you put it back on the gas ring'. (**Compton, Mackenzie, Beverley**)

Royal cats

The British Royal Family, it appears, have never been great cat lovers, ankle-high dogs from Wales seeming to be the current fashion in animal regalia. Indeed, when Elizabeth I was crowned the triumphal procession included an effigy of the Pope made of wicker in which were imprisoned dozens of live cats — the climax to the ceremony was the burning of the dummy, cats and all...

However, there have been notable exceptions, of course. It

was, after all, Queen Anne that the pussycat had been up to London to see in the nursery rhyme, and Charles I had a lucky black cat. When it died he declared that his luck had now gone — never a truer word was said, as the following day Cromwell's officers arrested him and he was later beheaded.

Queen Victoria was an ardent ailurophile. As well as being one of the most fervent supporters of the National Cat Club she also possessed two Blue Persians, one of which, **White Heather**, was inherited by her son Edward VII on her death. (*Anne*, *Charles*, *Victoria*, *Edward*)

Laura's rival

The great Italian lyric poet of the Renaissance, Petrarch, best known for his verses inspired by his beloved Laura, was also devoted to his cat. And when he retired to Arqua after Laura's death his cat was his only comfort. When Petrarch died the cat was embalmed and set in a niche in his study and beneath it a marble slab was inscribed with the words 'Second only to Laura'. (*Petrarch*, *Laura*)

Rumpelstilzchen ... etc.

Probably the most outrageous name for a cat must be that invented by Robert Southey, one-time Poet Laureate and friend of Wordsworth and Coleridge. Of his dozen or so cats which enjoyed such colourful tags as **Bona Marietta**, **The Zombi**, **Pulcheria** and **Sir Thomas Dido**, one stands out above all others: **Rumpelstilzchen, Marquis Macbum, Earl Tomlemange, Baron Raticide, Waowhler and Skaratch**! Rumpelstilzchen (for short) was left behind when Southey's neighbours at Greta Hall, Keswick, moved out, and the poet had just finished reading the story of Rumpelstiltskin to his children when the cat put its head around the door — and hence the name. Tabby and white with eyes a shade between chrysolite and emerald, Rumpelstilzchen was said not to be a

beautiful cat but one of truly gentlemanly bearing — though when it was discovered that he spent his formative years as a kitten in a bumbailiff's house the patronymic Macbum was added. Indoors Rumpelstilzchen reigned supreme in the Southey household but the garden was the domain of his archrival **Hurlyburlypuss**. When Rumpelstilzchen died he was buried in the orchard with catmint on his grave.

A great lover of cats, Southey once wrote that 'A kitten is in the animal world what a rosebud is in a garden.' (**Samuel**, **Mark**, **Southey**, **Robert**, **Greta**)

Presidential pussies

Mention is made elsewhere of the Washingtons' Mount Vernon cats, and Roosevelt's **Slippers** and **Tom Quartz**, but a number of other US heads of state have also befriended cats to such an extent that a love of the creatures almost seems a prerequisite for holding the office.

Calvin Coolidge had a grey-striped stray called **Tiger** that used to like to be slung around the President's neck as he walked about the White House and Abraham Lincoln's son, Tad, kept a cat called **Tabby**. In more recent times the Siamese appears to have been the more popular breed as both Susan Ford and Amy Carter owned examples — named **Shan** and **Misty Malarky Ying Yang** respectively. And Caroline Kennedy's cat was named after the Beatrix Potter character **Tom Kitten**. Ronald Reagan evidently also likes cats as when he was governor of California he even passed a law in 1973 giving prison sentences for anyone who kicked and injured other people's cats — with qualifications like that how could he fail to become president! (**Washington**, **Roosevelt**, **Coolidge**, **Tad**, **Amy**, **Ronald**, **Reagan**)

Cats at the top

Cats, it seems, are never far from the seat of power. Indeed, in the case of Cardinal Wolsey's black cat they were actually in it. For tradition holds that Henry VIII's influential Lord Chancellor always had his feline companion at his side when pronouncing judgements on matters of state. Catherine the Great, Empress of all the Russias, had a kitten presented to her by Prince Potemkin which she described as 'gay, witty and not obstinate' and in more recent times British Prime Minister George Canning even wrote verse in honour of his cat. Mussolini had a Persian and the French President Raymond Poincaré had a Siamese called **Gri-Gri**. Hindenburg said 'I cannot imagine a pleasant retired life of peace and meditation without a cat in the house' and the Great War statesman Georges 'The Tiger' Clemenceau took a black cat away with him after the 1919 conference of the Allies in London. Its name: **Prudence**. (**Wolsey**, **Potemkin**, **Canning**, **Benito**, **Raymond**, **Hindenburg**, **Clemenceau**)

The Rev. Dr John Langbourne, cat

The English philosopher Jeremy Bentham remembered as a child throwing a cat out of the window to see if it really did have nine lives. As it fell it turned towards him and with a mixture of fear and reproach mewed at him. This vision stayed with Bentham all his life and may account in part for his devotion to the cat of his adult days. The macaroni-eating **Sir John Langbourne** was apparently a profligate and frisky cat in his youth but as he grew older so he became more sedate and thoughtful and took to going to church. This decided Bentham that the cat should lay down his title and become the Rev. John Langbourne, and as his reputation for learning and sanctity grew he conferred on him a doctorate. When he died, Bentham said, the general opinion was that he was 'not far off a mitre'. The sacred body

was buried in a cemetery in Milton's garden. Bentham donated his own body to science and asked for his skeleton, wearing his clothes and surmounted by a wax replica of his head, to be put on public display. It can still be seen in University College, London. (**Bentham, Jeremy, Milton**)

GREYS, BLUES
AND SILVERS

Akela — The great grey wolf in Kipling's *The Jungle Book*.

Arethusa — After the legendary fountain in Ortygia. (*Ortygia*)

Ashputtel — The grey-clothed girl who slept in the ashes in the Grimms' Cinderella-like tale of the same name.

Aster/Astra — A star.

Belaud/du Bellay — After the silver-grey cat belonging to French poet Joachim du Bellay (see *Fictional Cats*). (*Joachim*)

Bellarmine — A fat-bellied jug, also called a greybeard, for a cat with both these qualities.

Benny — After Benny the Ball, the fat blue cat in TV's *Top Cat* (see *Comical Cats*).

Blighty — For a blue-blooded Brit of a cat.

Bluebell — The name of a South African Persian which produced one of the biggest litters on record — 14 kittens in 1974.

Bluebottle — A Goon of a cat which likes chasing flies? (*Goon*)

Bluey — Also the Australian word for a blanket, so for a blue cat that sleeps on one?

Boatswain/Bosun — A navy-blue cat (Byron had a dog of this name). (*Byron*)

Borage — A courageous cat, after the blue-flowered plant: 'I Borage bring always courage' (Pliny).

Borak — Meaning 'lightning'.

Bugle — A blue wildflower and perhaps for a strident cat.

Bullet — A silver-grey cat that's as quick as a shot.

Carlton/Carruthers — For another true-blue cat (members of the British Conservative Party frequent the Carlton Club in London's St James's).

Celesta/Celeste — From the Latin for 'heavenly', for a cat the colour of the sky. Also after the tinkling keyboard instrument.

Chalcedony — A greyish kind of quartz.

Champagne — A sparkling silver-white cat that brings out the best in people.

Chateaubriand — After the cat-loving writer who adopted the grey-and-red Micetto (q.v.).

Cobby — (See *Physical Characteristics*.)

Copacabana — After the long silver-sand beach in Rio de Janeiro.

Dollar — A silver-dollar cat.

Dorian — After Dorian Gray, the character in Oscar Wilde's novel who never seems to grow old.

Dusty — A grey-haired cat or one that just likes getting dirty. Also after Dusty the great mother who produced 420 babies! (See *Record-Breaking Cats*.)

Dynamite — A dangerous type.

Earl — After the politician Earl Grey, for whom the bergamot-flavoured tea is named.

Elegy — Thomas Gray (1716-71) wrote the 'Elegy written in a Country Churchyard' and an ode on the death of Horace Walpole's cat Selima (see *Cats of the Famous*). (*Horace*)

Eminence — For an *eminence grise* or a cat that wields power behind the scenes. The original 'grey eminence' was Père Joseph, secretary to Cardinal Richelieu, who was himself a great cat-lover (see *Cats of the Famous*). (*Joseph*)

Esprit — French for 'spirit', for a lively cat.

Ferris — From the Latin *ferrum*, meaning 'iron', and also for a big wheel of a cat?

Flash — A brilliant, speedy or ostentatious cat.

Foggy — For a smoky-grey cat. Also perhaps 'Willy' after Willy Fog, a top-hatted English Victorian gentleman lion who appears in the animated cartoon series *Around the World with Willy Fog,* based on Jules Verne's story *Around the World in Eighty Days.* (*Jules*)

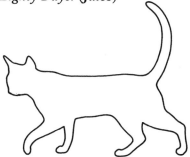

Forget-me-not — A pretty blue flower also called 'scorpion grass' — for a cat with a sting in its tail you are bound to remember.

Frazier — After a silver Persian from Houston, Texas, which was a finalist in the All-American Glamor Katz Contest in 1974 and who could reputedly play the piano...

Frosty — (See *Exotics and Rare Breeds*.)

Grace — For a cat whose colours are greys, also after Orlando the Marmalade Cat's partner in the Kathleen Hale stories.

Grampus — After the common slate-grey dolphin (also the name of a killer whale, so perhaps too for a vicious black-and-white cat).

Grimalkin — An old cat, especially a female one (from 'grey malkin' an archaic word for a cat).

Grimes — For a grimy grey or black cat.

Grisaille — A style of painting in shades of grey, so for a grey-streaked or tabby cat.

Grisette — After the grey dress fabric once worn by French working girls, especially flirtatious ones — for a flirty feline.

Harvey — The name of a five-month-old smoky Persian who featured on BBC TV's main news when he survived 10 minutes inside a fully loaded washing-machine.

Hester — From the Greek for a star.

Hyacinth — For a blue or white variety.

Hyssop — After the aromatic blue-flowered plant.

Iolanthe — From the Greek for 'violet'.

John Peel — 'D'ye ken John Peel with his coat so grey...'

Juan — After Juan Gris (grey) the Spanish cubist painter.

Juno — Classical goddess of the silvery moon and Roman queen of the Olympian gods. So for one with regal beauty and a stately bearing.

Lady Jane — After Lady Jane Grey, and the savage cat in Dickens's *Bleak House* (see *Cats of the Famous*).

Lambkin — Silver Lambkin was an enormous Chinchilla that on his death was stuffed and put on show in London's Natural History Museum.

Leucos — Greek for 'grey' (also one of Actaeon's hounds).

Lightning — A cat like a powerful flash of white light, also for a blue, after the American blues singer, Lightning Hopkins. (*Hopkins*)

Lincoln — A stately Union-blue cat.

Lloyd — A Celtic name meaning 'grey'.

Long John — After Long John Silver. Perhaps also for a three-legged type with a patch over one eye, or even one that seems to be wearing thermal underwear? (*Silver*)

Luna — Italian goddess of the moon.

Lupin — After the (commonly blue) plant, from the Latin for a wolf, so perhaps also for a ravenous cat?

Maud — Maud was a shawl or rug of grey wool formerly worn in Scotland — perhaps also for a cat that likes to come into the garden?

Mercury/Hermes — A quicksilver cat. (Hermes had a tortoiseshell lyre so maybe also for a tortie?)

Micetto — After Pope Leo XII's grey-and-red cat banded with black (see *Cats of the Famous*).

Misty — A hazy grey cat (see also *Exotics and Rare Breeds*).

Mojo — A cat that doesn't like strangers? ('Got my mojo working but it just don't work on you...' as the song goes.)

Moko — After the blue Maori tattoo.

Mouche — After Huysmans's green-eyed grey (see *Cats of the Famous*).

Muddy Waters — A muddy-grey puss, or a blue one after the great blues guitarist of this name.

Mushroom — For a cat that suddenly appears from nowhere?

Nicky/Nike — For a triumphant nickel-coloured cat (*nike* is Greek for 'victory').

Nimbus — A dark-grey cloud.

Ozone — Ozone is blue.

Percheron — After the heavy grey carthorse.

Periwinkle — A pretty blue wildflower.

Pewter — A versatile cat the colour of this grey lead alloy.

Phoebe — A Titaness who became goddess of the silvery moon.

Platinum — For a very valuable silver-grey cat.

Portland — A cement-grey type.

Pusha — A cat-like Russian name (a variant of Pavel), for a Russian Blue? (**Pavel**)

Ray — For a little ray of sunshine.

Reckitt — For a blue.

Rocky — For a rock-coloured cat or a particularly pugnacious puss.

Scintilla — A scintillating feline.

Selene — Greek goddess of the moon.

Serge — For a blue cat, after the cloth.

Shadow — A dark cat that follows you around.

Shale/Shingles — After the silver-grey rock and gravel forms.

Silverado — The title of a film.

Sindbad — An adventurous, sailor-blue cat.

Sky — A cat the colour of the firmament.

Slippers — After Teddy Roosevelt's six-toed White House cat.

Smoky — A good name for a Smoke Oriental Shorthair or indeed for any smoky old cat. US President Coolidge was once given a bobcat called Smoky. (*Coolidge*)

Smudge — For a soft grey.

Soda — A fizzy type.

Southampton — After Shakespeare's friend the Earl of Southampton who owned a blue-and-white short-haired cat.

Sparky — A bright cat or one who is the crème de la crème, after Muriel Spark who wrote *The Prime of Miss Jean Brodie*.

Squill — After the plant with blue flowers.

Stannard — From the Latin word for 'tin'.

Steel — A tough but flexible blue or grey cat.

Storm — For a quarrelsome dark grey puss.

Tarpan — After the grey wild horse.

Tinsel — A sparkling, festive type.

Twinkle/Twink/Twinkie — For the twinkle in your eye.

Ultramar — An ultramarine blue cat.

Vashti — The word for a star in Persian.

Vivian — The Lady of the Lake and mistress of Merlin in Arthurian legend. A lake-blue cat.

Wedgwood — For a blue or blue-and-white cat, after the pottery.

Zafiro — Spanish for 'sapphire'.

Zaza — The pale grey female cat in the *Hector's House* children's TV animated puppet series first broadcast in 1965. Hector was the rather slow-witted brown dog ('I'm a great big stupid old Hector') and their other friend was Kiki the Frog. For a slightly prissy pussy. (**Hector**, **Kiki**)

Zinco — For a zinc-coloured cat.

Zizi — A silver-grey cat owned by Théophile Gautier.

CATS IN THE ARTS

Cat painters

An enormous number of artists have, perhaps understandably, been drawn to depicting the feline form over the years and many of these are mentioned elsewhere. Whistler, who himself owned a brown, gold and white cat, made sketches of the French poet Mallarmé's jet-black **Lilith**, and painters from Sir Joshua Reynolds and Dürer to Gwen John, and from Renoir and Manet to Picasso have all daubed out portraits of pussies. Indeed, cats have often eclipsed other subjects on the same canvas, as in Hockney's *Mr and Mrs Clark and Percy*. Specialists in cat painting have included Gottfried Mind, Henriette Ronner and Théophile Steinlen, but perhaps the best known British exponent was Louis Wain.

Born in the West End of London in 1860, Louis Wain originally trained as a musician but his life changed at the age of 21 when he was given a black-and-white cat called **Peter**. He was so taken by this creature that he decided to paint its portrait and the rest, as they say, is history. Through such works as *Madam Tabethy's Academy* and *Cats' Christmas Party* — not to mention sales of *The Louis Wain Annual* — he rapidly became world-famous and extremely wealthy. However, fame and fortune didn't make him turn his back on his feline friends and when Harrison Weir retired as first president of the National Cat Club he accepted the post, and though his later years were spent in a psychiatric hospital, he none the less continued to paint cats to the very end. (**Whistler**, *Steinlen*, *Joshua*, *Albrecht*, *Gwen*, *Auguste*, *Pablo*, *Hogarth*, *Gottfried*, *Henriette*, *Louis*, *Tabethy*)

Operatic cats

No doubt to a feline ear the nocturnal caterwauling of their fellows is high art, but to the average human anxious to indulge in some hard-earned rest the only fee such backyard buskers are likely to receive is a well-aimed boot or the contents of a bucket of cold water. However, remarkable though it may seem, two of the world's finest composers have been so inspired by the racket that they have produced classical duets for male and female voices. Ravel's opera *L'Enfant et les Sortilèges*, features one, with a libretto written by cat-lover Colette, while the hilarious *Duetto Buffo di Due Gatti* by Giacchino Rossini has attracted such international star performers as Victoria de los Angeles and Elisabeth Schwarzkopf. (**Maurice**, **Giacchino**, **Rossini**)

The Raphael of cats

The undisputed master of cat portraiture was the Swiss painter Gottfried Mind (1768-1814), born in Berne of Hungarian parents. Mind's pictures were so popular that there was a constant demand for his work throughout his lifetime — some of his paintings even finding their way into the royal palaces of Europe. And his talents weren't confined to the easel as he also did a roaring trade in miniature feline sculptures exquisitely carved out of chestnuts.

His own favourite cat, **Minette**, used to sit on his lap while he worked, checking every detail, and more often than not two or three kittens would perch on his shoulders and peer curiously down as the paintings took shape. However, Minette and the rest of his menagerie of cats nearly came to a sticky end in 1809. When a rabies epidemic broke out in Switzerland that year the police ordered the destruction of 800 cats in a desperate measure to halt the spread of the disease. By a miracle, the artist managed to rescue his pets from the authorities just in time — a case, perhaps, of Mind over matter?

Keyboard cats

One of the most famous examples of cat music is Scarlatti's *Cat Fugue*, supposedly inspired by the sounds produced when the composer's inquisitive pet walked over the keys of his harpsichord — what a 'helpful' kitten could do with a modern synthesizer makes the mind boggle. (**Scarlatti, Domenico**)

Heraldic cats

Probably because its independent spirit seemed to embody the very principle of freedom, the cat was widely used as a symbol of liberty in ancient times and frequently appeared on shields and banners as well as coats of arms. And the statue of the Goddess of Liberty herself has a cat at her feet. The Roman army employed a number of cat devices — for example the green cat on a silver background borne by the solders of the Ordini Augusti company — and the Suevi, Vandals, Alani and Dutch all used the symbol of the sable cat on their battle flags. Indeed, it is even thought that the three leopards that form part of the British Royal Arms were originally cats.

Many noble European dynasties have also used the cat device — both the German Katzen and the Italian Della Gatta families having a silver cat on an azure background in their coats of arms. And the Scottish Mackintosh clan have as their motto 'Touch not the cat but [i.e. without] a glove'. Which serves to remind us that Napoleon's dictum about the iron fist in a velvet glove is exactly replicated in a cat's paw. (**Ordini, Suevi, Vandal, Alani, Mackintosh**)

Dancing cats

One of the most successful stage musicals ever must be *Cats* based on T.S. Eliot's book of poems, *Old Possum's Book of Practical Cats,* and with music by Andrew Lloyd Webber. With choreography by Gillian Lynne and the striking designs of John

Napier, the show began at the New London Theatre under director Trevor Nunn before opening at the Winter Gardens in New York on 7 October 1982.

The tales of Beatrix Potter were also adapted for ballet with all the well-named Potter cat characters such as **Simpkin** and **Mrs Tabitha Twitchit**. And in Tchaikovsky's *Sleeping Beauty* there is a *pas de deux* danced by Puss in Boots and the White Cat while the orchestra imitates cat sounds.

But for the ultimate dancing cat experience, nothing beats the real McCoy. American choreographer, George Balanchine, who once said that he preferred cats to people, even taught his own white-and-ginger cat **Mourka** to do *jetés* and *tours en l'air* — now *that's* dancing! (**Stearns, Webber, Andrew, Lloyd, Trevor, Balanchine**)

A cat Nell Gwynne

The celebrated 18th-century English painter and engraver William Hogarth included cats in a number of his works. Tabbies appear in *The Industrial Apprentice*, *Hudibras* and others and a white cat features in Scene 3 of the famous *The Harlot's Progress* sequence. However, perhaps the most memorable of all his cat paintings occurs in the otherwise rather dull group portrait, *The Graham Children*. Indeed, the distinguished art historian and critic Sir Kenneth Clark was so impressed by this creature that he described her as 'the embodiment of cockney vitality, alert and adventurous…A Nell Gwynne amongst cats' — besides which the Graham children looked 'hollow and lifeless'. (**Hudibras, Kenneth, Nell, Graham**)

Pottery pussies?

Cat figurines have been made out of all varieties of pottery, from Meissen to Chelsea, from Derby to Delft and from Staffordshire to the ever popular Goss. But perhaps the most common pottery *image* of a cat is that of **Maneki-Neko**, the

Japanese good-luck cat, which sits in the windows of Japanese homes, shops and restaurants all over the world and whose image adorns the temple of Go-To-Ku-Ji. Legend has it that long ago the temple was in a very poor condition — times were hard and sacrifices had to be made, but at least it kept its temple cat. One day, as a band of samurai warriors was passing by, one of the soldiers saw the cat washing herself with her paw over her ear and thought that she was waving welcome. As a result the samurai went into the temple and were well entertained by the Buddhist priests despite their poverty. Indeed, so impressed was one of the warriors by their generosity that he later returned for religious instruction and when he died gave a large endowment to the temple.

The tricolour pottery Maneki-Neko — or 'beckoning cat' — sits on its haunches with one front paw raised to its ear and the other holding a coin, symbolizing prosperity. This link between pottery, cats and money can also, coincidentally, be found embodied in the valuable porcelain artefacts made by Japan's mainland neighbour — 'ming' is the Chinese word for 'miaow'! (*Go-To-Ku-Ji*, *Ming*)

A tapestry cat

Hanging in Mary Queen of Scots' bedroom in Holyrood Palace, Edinburgh, is a tapestry embroidered by the queen's own hand depicting a cat and mouse which is believed to symbolize the relationship between the ill-fated Scottish royal and Elizabeth I of England, who played cat and mouse with her for years before finally having her executed. (*Mary*)

Holy cats

In some Christian legends a cat gave birth to kittens in the Bethlehem stable at exactly the same moment that Jesus was born to Mary. And as the Virgin held the holy child in her arms the inquisitive cat is supposed to have come up to inspect the

new arrival. However, fearing that her face was too close to the baby, Mary gently pushed her head away and where her fingers touched, an 'M' for 'Mary' was left impressed between the cat's ears, which still remains to this day.

Indeed, it is strange that there is no mention of cats anywhere in the Bible, but as if to make up for this oversight a great many artists have included feline figures in their paintings of Christian scenes. Leonardo, Barocci and Rembrandt have all produced portraits of the Virgin and Child with cats, for example, and Dürer and Bosch's Adam and Eve in Eden scenes have included them — watching a mouse and eating a tadpole, respectively. Some pictures, however, use the image of a cat as a symbol of perfidy and in paintings of the Last Supper, like the one by Raphael, the cat appears at the feet of Judas Iscariot. (*Raphael*, *Judas*, *Leonardo*, *Baroccio*, *Rembrandt*, *Hieronymous*)

Cat concertos

Brueghel's famous picture of the cat's concert is not so fanciful as some might think. In the 19th century a *concert miaulant* was held in Paris with several cats ranged in a row and a monkey as conductor, and earlier examples have been recorded. However, a less pleasant attempt at utilizing the feline vocal chords was made in Brussels in 1549 at a festival in honour of King Philip II. On one of the floats in the procession was a 'cat organ' comprising 20 hapless pussies confined side by side in narrow cases with their tails sticking out the top and tied by strings to a keyboard. As a bear depressed the keys the cats' tails would be yanked by strings and their owners would yelp in pain.

A far more efficient and less distressing way of incorporating cat voices into orchestral music was found by Prokofiev whose *Peter and the Wolf* suite makes use of a clarinet to convey the sound, as does the *Berceuses du Chat* by Stravinsky. (*Brueghel*, *Stravinsky*, *Igor*)

Ecclesiastical cats

Because of their supposed satanic associations cats have not featured as regularly in church architecture as some other, more 'holy' animals. None the less, a number have managed to slink in, mostly as wood carvings on bench-ends in choirstalls or as decorations on misericords. Particularly fine examples of these can be found in Beverley Minster and Winchester, Wells, Exeter and Hereford cathedrals, and overseas in such churches as San Giorgio Maggiore in Venice and on a pillar in Rouen Cathedral. St Albans Church in High Holborn, London, is unique in possessing a stone statue of a cat, which 'supervised' the builders' works but didn't live to see its completion. But perhaps most remarkable of all is the headstone to '"The Church Cat" 1912-1927' in the graveyard of St Mary Redcliffe Church, Bristol. Formerly known as **Tommy**, the cat, originally a stray, just moved into the church one day and was fed every night by the verger. A popular attraction with the congregations, he certainly must have had a very saintly demeanour to have been buried in such hallowed ground.

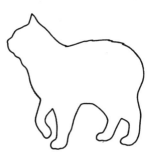

GINGERS, ORANGES AND BROWNS

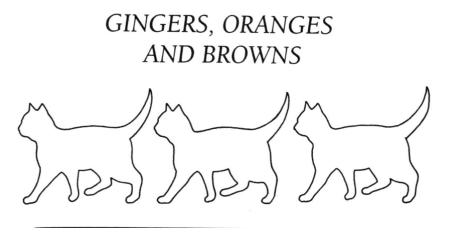

Amber — After the star of the film *The Cat from Outer Space* (see *Screen Cats*).

Antigone — (See *Exotics and Rare Breeds.*)

Aubade — For an orange cat that sings at dawn, after the song.

Aurora — Roman goddess of the dawn.

Baccy/Baci — For a tobacco-coloured cat, or one that kisses you a lot (*baci* are kisses in Italian).

Barbarossa — Meaning 'red-beard' and also after Frederick Barbarossa (1123-90), Holy Roman Emperor and King of Germany. (**Frederick**)

Baroness — (See *Exotics and Rare Breeds.*)

Bay/Bayard — For a reddish brown, bay-coloured cat — also after the fearless and irreproachable French knight, the Chevalier de Bayard (1473-1524).

Beech — A copper-coloured cat.

Beach — For a sandy variety and after Lord Emsworth's butler in the P.G. Wodehouse stories. (**Emsworth**)

Betony — A reddish-purple plant.

Billy — After a ginger-and-white tom that used to bang the

knocker of its owners' door to be let in (see *A Cat Miscellany*).

Biscuit/Bisque — For a pale brown cookie cat.

Bourneville — A chocolate-coloured type.

Brandy — From the Dutch for 'burnt wine' — for a cat that's hot stuff.

Brooke/Lipton/Ty-Phoo — Tea-coloured cats. (Ty-Phoo for an oriental brown perhaps?)

Brownie — A small nutty chocolate puss.

Bruno — An Italian name meaning 'with brown hair'.

Buffy/Buffo — For a buff-coloured cat and also after the French naturalist who took a particular interest in cats, the Comte de Buffon (1707-88). *Buffo* is Italian for 'comic'.

Buttercup — A blood-donor tom that saved other cats' lives (see *Cats of the Famous*).

Butterscotch — A sweet pale brown type.

Caesar — For any ginger cat (Julius Caesar had red hair) but particular for those with Roman noses, such as the Rex varieties. (*Julius*)

Capability — After Lancelot 'Capability' Brown, the famous landscape gardener — for a cat that likes rearranging the garden... (*Lancelot*)

Cappuccino — A milky coffee-coloured type.

Castana — Spanish for 'chestnut'. Hence 'castanets', a good name for a musical cat of this colour.

Chestnut — For any brown type, but particularly a Havana Brown, as the name they were first known by in the UK was Chestnut Brown Foreign.

Clementine — A darling cat the colour of this fruit.

Cob — Another name for the hazelnut.

Coco — For a cocoa-coloured cat, or a slinky Coco Chanel-style pussy. Also after Ccoa, the malevolent feline spirit feared by the Quicha Indians of ancient Peru as the bringer of hail and lightning which destroyed the crops — for a particularly destructive type. Alternatively, after *coco*, the Portuguese word for 'grimace' from which the coconut gets its name (the three holes look like a face). Thus a grinning moggy who's a bit of a clown? (**Chanel**, **Quicha**)

Coffee — A stimulating pick-me-up pussy. Also doubly appropriate for a cat of this hue as in olden times hardened drinkers referred to tea and coffee as 'catlap'.

Cointreau — After the orange liqueur.

Conker — For an all-conquering chestnut.

Cookie — A mad brown cat with chocolate spots.

Copernicus — A cat that likes star-gazing, or one with copper knickers!

Coral — For a pale brown one with a very pink nose and tongue...

Cornelius — After cornelian (or carnelian), a reddish yellow gemstone.

Dandelion — For a yellow cat with lion's teeth! (The dandelion is named from the shape of its leaves: *dent de lion* is French for 'tooth of a lion'.)

Darjeeling — A tea-coloured cat.

Dawn — After the celebrated Red Self Persian known as **Pathfinders** Golden Dawn, or less generously, for a cat that wakes you up at 6 a.m.!

Demerara — A little brown sugar...

Derby/Trilby — Cockney rhyming slang for a cat is 'brown hat', so why not name him after a brown bowler hat —known in the USA as a derby — or a trilby? The word 'trilby', incidentally, was invented by George du Maurier in the book of the same name for the eponymous heroine who trilled a lot — very suitable for a noisy cat.

Donald — Gaelic for 'a brown stranger'.

Eos — Greek goddess of the dawn.

Espresso — A speedy, dark coffee-coloured variety.

Evelyn — Meaning 'hazel'.

Fag — A tobacco-coloured cat — or one that is particularly servile.

Fidel — For a Havana Brown, after Fidel Castro, the ruler of Cuba, or for any faithful cat (*fidel* means 'faithful'). (*Castro*)

Flapjack — After the oat biscuit.

Foxy — Foxing produces brown spots on old paper, also perhaps for a cunning cat.

Fozzie — Fozzie was the unsuccessful stand-up comic brown bear in *The Muppets* TV series.

Freckles — For a pale brown type with darker brown spots.

Freddy — After the unnamed cat owned by Fat Freddy of the Fabulous Furry Freak Brothers. This extraordinary laid-back orange cat rose to fame in the days of Underground comics and now has his own series of magazines drawn by Gilbert Shelton and Dave Sheridan, which have a cult following. (*Shelton*, *Sheridan*)

Fuchsia — A showy plant with flowers in various colours, including red and white — for a flashy cat.

Fudge — A soft, sweet brown delicacy.

Gaea/Gaia/Ge — The great Earth mother in Greek myth, so for a maternal brown.

Galanthis — After the servant of the Queen of Thebes in Ovid's *Metamorphoses* who is turned into a cat (see *Legendary Cats*).

Garibaldi/Garry — A pale brown cat with darker spots, after the biscuit. Or perhaps for a hairless type?

Gazpacho — Gazpacho is a cold Spanish soup made from tomatoes, peppers etc. — for a cool ruddy cat.

Gilroy — From the Gaelic, meaning 'red-headed servant'.

Ginger — After a curious cat who features in the records of the London Patent Office (see *Top Cats*).

Gingersnap/Gingernut — For crisp, snappy types.

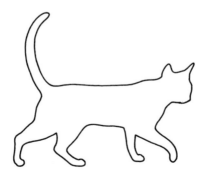

Hadrian — After the great Roman emperor, whose name means 'dark one'.

Havana — For a Havana Brown or any other cigar-coloured type.

Hazel — For a nutty brown cat, or one with hazel eyes.

Heather/Ling — Two names for the reddish-purple shrub.

Henna — An auburn type.

Hobbes — A toy tiger that becomes real in the fantasies of little boy Calvin in the bestselling books based on the comic strip *Calvin and Hobbes*, created by Bill Watterson. (*Calvin*, *Bill*, *Watterson*)

Jasper — One of the forms of this crystalline quartz is brown in colour.

Jinx — Mr Jinx was the unfortunate orange cat in *Pixie and Dixie* that 'hates those meeces to pieces'. Jinx was also the 'reckless swashbuckler' companion of Freddy the pig in the series of books by Walter Brooks.

Jock — After a ginger cat owned by Winston Churchill.

Jonesey — Sigourney Weaver's ginger cat in the film *Aliens*. (*Sigourney*)

Jubby — *Acinonyx jubatus* is the Latin name for a cheetah, so for any black-spotted pale brown type.

Kit — Have a break, get a Kit-Kat!

Lapsang Souchong — For an oriental tea-coloured breed that sits on your lap?

Leander/Leandra/Lionel — Good regal cat names meaning 'lion like'. Leander was also the lover of Hero, the priestess of Aphrodite, in the ancient story told by Ovid. Every night he would swim across the Hellespont to visit her, until one day a storm blew out her guiding lantern and he was drowned. For particularly romantic cats. (*Aphrodite*)

Leicester/Lester — Perhaps for a cheese-eating cat the colour of Red Leicester?

Lenny — Lenny the Lion was a well-known TV personality in Britain in the 1960s controlled, with difficulty, by ventriloquist Terry Hall. (*Terry*)

Leo — Latin for 'lion' and the name of the one that roars at the beginning of every MGM film. The role has been played by many lions over the years, the first being **Slats** and the first in Technicolor being **Tanner**. **Jackie** (actually a male lion) played the part for nearly 18 years and also appeared in over 250 films. (He was named after Jacqueline Logan, the leading lady of his tenth feature, *Burning Sands* [1922].)

Leonardo — After Leonardo the Lion from Nowhere in a children's book of the same name by Adrian Mitchell. Perhaps also for a very inventive cat? (*Mitchell*)

Llewellyn — 'Lion-like' or 'lightning'.

Lucy — After Lucille Ball, the auburn-haired US comedienne.

Macavity — The 'Mystery Cat' in *Old Possum's Book* by T.S. Eliot.

Madame Théophile — After one of the most devoted of French writer Théophile Gautier's nine cats (see *Cats of the Famous*).

Malteser -- For a brown-and-white cat, after the sweet, and perhaps also for a Russian Blue, which were formerly known as Maltese cats.

Mandarin — For an orange cat, or for an inscrutable one whose power is such that he seems to be a law unto himself, like the Chinese mandarins.

Marigold — Any yellow/orange puss, after the flower, but also after the cat immortalized in a poem by Richard Garnett.

Marmite — A dark brown type.

Mavis — Another name for the songthrush — so for a cat with these markings.

Melba — A peach of an orangey puss.

Morris — The 15lb orange-striped star of the 9-Lives catfood commercials in the USA (see *Screen Cats*).

Muffin — A brown cake in the USA, a white bread in the UK.

Mulligatawny/Mulligan — For a spicy brown cat, after the curry-flavoured soup.

Naranja — Spanish for 'orange'.

Nissa — The real name of the pet leopard called **Baby** in the film *Bringing up Baby* (1930) starring Cary Grant and Katharine Hepburn. Baby gets lost but is eventually retrieved. (*Cary*, *Katharine*)

Noble — After the lion king in the 12th-century story of Reynard the Fox, who is tricked by the wily fox.

Norman — After the leopards that appear in the British Royal Arms, two of which are from Normandy, the third being from Guienne.

Nugget — A little bundle of pure gold.

Nutmeg/Mace — After the musky culinary seed.

Ocker — For an ochre cat.

Olé/Ollie — For a café-au-lait-coloured kitty!

Orangey — An Oscar-winning cat, star of *Rhubarb* and *Breakfast at Tiffany's* (see *Screen Cats*).

Oren — Welsh for 'orange'.

Outspan — For an orange cat.

Pardo — The Spanish word for 'brown' (also for a leopard).

Parsley — Parsley is the lion in Michael Bond's delightful children's TV animated puppet series, *The Adventures of Parsley,* derived from the earlier *The Herbs*. His great friend is Dill the dog. (**Michael, Dill**)

Pears — After the translucent, aromatic soap and perhaps also for a singing cat, after the tenor Peter Pears.

Pekoe — Broken orange pekoe is a type of tea — for a brown or orange cat that always appears at tea-time...

Pepsi — For a fizzy brown type.

Pippin — After the superior British apple, the Cox's Orange Pippin.

Pomander — For an orange cat with clove-brown spots.

Pomelo — A yellow-orange grapefruit-like fruit.

Porphyria — After the red/purple stone, porphyry.

Reddy — The little ginger cat in Hanna-Barbera's first animated TV series, *The Ruff and Reddy Show* (1957), which led to the hugely successful *Huckleberry Hound Show* (Ruff was a large dog).

Reynard — A foxy brown cat.

Richard — For a lion-hearted type, after Richard I of England.

Rory — From the Irish Gaelic meaning 'red king'. Or possibly for a lion-hearted Siamese or other 'talking' breeds?

Rufus — The Latin word for 'red-haired'.

Rusty — A very suitable name for a ginger cat.

Sable — A sable-coloured cat.

Saffron — An orange-yellow colour derived from a kind of crocus of this name.

Sahara/Sandy — For a ginger or sandy-coloured type.

Sarsaparilla — A dark-red drink made from the roots of the smilax plant. (**Smilax**)

Scrumpy — For a scrumptious brown cat, with a hard, rough edge, after the West Country cider.

Shammy — A chamois-coloured puss.

Shandy — Either a pale brown cat or one that is brown and white like the ingredients of the drink: beer and lemonade. Alternatively, for one that never finishes anything, after Tristram Shandy in Sterne's novel. (*Tristram*)

Sherry/Whisky/Cider/Calvados/Beer/Porter — All good brown names.

Sika — A chestnut deer with white spots. Perhaps also for a constantly prowling type (seeker)?

Skimbleshanks — The railway cat with the long brown tail in T.S. Eliot's poem.

Sorrel — A light-brown or brownish-orange type.

Spice — Spice of Ridgefield, Connecticut, a ginger-and-white tom, was one of the heaviest cats on record, weighing in at 43lb before he died in 1977.

Spiro — A ginger owned by cat artist Lesley Anne Ivory.

Tangerine/Tangiers — An orangey puss ('tangerine' means 'from Tangiers').

Tealeaf — A brown, thieving cat (from Cockney rhyming slang).

Tinto — For a ruddy type (*vino tinto* is Spanish red wine).

Toast — A brown-and-white or brown and dark brown cat that's the toast of the town!

Tommy — After Tommy Clark of Seneca Falls, New York, a cat that held huge parties (see *Top Cats*).

Tonto — After Art Carney's co-star in the film *Harry and Tonto* (see *Screen Cats*).

Topaz — For a cat of this colour and after Taffy the Topaz Cat (see *Exotics and Rare Breeds*).

Umber/Humber — A dark earth colour.

Van Dyke — Van Dyke brown is a medium brown — also perhaps for a cat with large whiskers like the artist's moustache.

Vespa — Latin for 'wasp', so for a black-and-yellow hooped type.

Zebedee — After the bewhiskered, red-faced man on a spring who tells us when it is time for bed in TV's *Magic Roundabout* puppet series.

Zest — An invigorating cat, from the name for the peel of an orange.

FICTIONAL
CATS

Novel cats

No good novel could be complete without a cat. Dickens included several in his works and many classics have at least one. In Louisa M. Alcott's *Little Women* Amy's cat dies and she writes its epitaph, in Charlotte Brontë's *Shirley* one of Robert Moore's redeeming features is that he allows the cat to sleep on his knee (the Brontës themselves had a cat called **Tiger**); and, in more recent times, in Paul Gallico's *Jennie* a boy actually turns into a cat.

The French author Anatole France — winner of the Nobel Prize for Literature in 1921 — included his own real-life cat in his first successful novel, *Le Crime de Sylvestre Bonnard.* Evidently the cat kept a close eye on the creative process and knew when the plot was starting to waiver — every night when he felt it was time to go to bed he would knock the pen from his master's hand! (**Gallico, Jennie, Anatole**)

Puss-in-Boots, or the Master Cat

In Perrault's fairytale a miller dies and his sons share out the estate. The eldest has the mill, the second the donkey and the youngest is greatly disappointed to inherit only his father's cat, believing that he'll starve to death as a result. However, the cat overhears this and says that if he will only give him a sack and a pair of boots to protect him from brambles, all will be well. Knowing that this cat is cleverer than most, he agrees and by various ruses the cat manages to trap a number of wild animals,

taking each to the King as a gift from his master, whom he describes as the Marquis of Carabas. One day the King and his beautiful daughter are driving along the riverbank when the cat has the idea of making his master pretend he is drowning. When the royal party learn that the Marquis of Carabas is in trouble, the King remembers his gifts and orders him to be rescued, dressing him in the finest clothes as his own have apparently been stolen (in reality hidden by the cat). Attracting the princess's eye now in his finery, he is invited into the coach and everywhere they journey the local farmhands declare that they are working on the Marquis of Carabas's estate, having been threatened earlier by the cat. The cat, meanwhile, has discovered that the real owner of the lands, a hideous ogre, is able to change into any kind of animal, and tricks him into turning into a mouse which he subsequently eats. Thus, when the King arrives at the ogre's castle he is greeted by the cat who declares it to be the Marquis's home. Later, over a feast prepared earlier for some of the ogre's friends, the King offers his daughter's hand in marriage to the miller's son. He accepts and they are wed the same day. For his part, the cat becomes a great lord and only chases mice for relaxation. A clever cat indeed. (**Perrault**, **Carabas**, **Marquis**)

The Cheshire cat

There is no such breed as a Cheshire cat, though the phrase 'to grin like a Cheshire cat' was common in Lewis Carroll's day and probably derived from the fact that Cheshire cheeses used to be made in the shape of a grinning cat. The Cheshire cat that Alice meets in *Alice's Adventures in Wonderland* first appears in the Duchess's kitchen in Chapter VI and is the only occupant of the room — apart from the Cook — who isn't constantly sneezing because of the vast amount of pepper used in the cooking. It later appears sitting in a tree and tells Alice the way before disappearing completely, starting with the tip of its tail and

ending with its grin which remains even after its body has gone. Later still, in Chapter VIII, it asks Alice how she's enjoying the Queen of Hearts's croquet match using flamingoes as mallets and hedgehogs as balls. Alice waits until its ears appear before answering, as it won't be able to hear her reply otherwise. Just as she's complaining about their cheating, the King and Queen appear and demand the cat's execution, but an argument then begins because of the impossibility of beheading a cat who has become merely a head. The cat solves the problem by fading away completely. (**Dodgson, Lutwidge, Lewis**)

Raminagrobis, the mighty judge

In Jean de La Fontaine's *Fables* the story of 'The Cat, the Weasel and the Young Rabbit' tells of a happy little rabbit called Jean who lived in an old burrow in the country and spent every day from dusk to dawn nibbling away in the surrounding clover fields to his heart's content.

One day, after a particularly satisfying meal, he returned to his burrow for a well-earned sleep when he discovered to his horror that an old lady weasel had occupied his ancestral home and refused to budge. Outraged, Jean threatened to summon his friends the rats to clear her out but the weasel insisted that it was empty when she arrived and so she had every right to occupy it, and that the fact that it had been in the rabbit's family for generations was irrelevant.

After much heated dispute they decided to put the matter to an independent arbiter and agreed to ask the wise old hermit cat, **Raminagrobis**, to settle the issue one way or the other. So away they went to find the great sage and when they had sought him out began to state their separate cases. However, before they could proceed far in their testimony, Raminagrobis held up a paw to interrupt them and explained that he was sorry, but the rigours of old age had affected his hearing and could they come closer and speak directly into his ears. Suspecting nothing, the simple creatures did as they were bid and approached him to clarify their predicament. However, no sooner were the rabbit and the weasel in striking distance than the wily old cat lashed out at both of them and with a sudden movement of his razor-sharp claws settled their dispute for good and proceeded to devour both litigants. (*La Fontaine*)

Saha, the co-respondent cat

Saha is the beautiful pure-bred Russian Blue cat in Colette's short story 'The Cat', first published in France in 1944. Alain Amparat, only son and heir to the Amparat Silks fortune, lives alone with his mother and his adored 'pearl-coloured demon' cat, Saha, bought at a cat-show when aged only five months. Life without Saha would be unthinkable for the young man, and when he becomes engaged to Camille Mangles he hopes the cat and her new mistress will get on well.

However, after the couple get married, Camille becomes increasingly jealous of Saha as time goes by and begins to feel that Alain is lavishing more affection on the cat than his wife, Finally, one day, in a fit of pique she pushes the cat off a sixth-floor balcony. Miraculously, the cat survives with only minor injuries but subsequently hisses at Camille whenever she comes near. Alain eventually guesses what has happened between the two women in his life and Camille gives him an ultimatum — either the cat goes or she does. The answer to Alain is clear, as Saha watches Camille depart . . . (*Alain, Amparat, Camille*)

A cat horror story

One of the grisliest cat stories is 'The Black Cat' by Edgar Allan Poe. Written in the form of a confession from a condemned man's cell it tells how the narrator once owned a large, beautiful and sagacious cat called **Pluto** who followed him everywhere

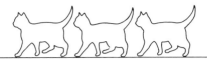

and was his favourite of all his many pets. However, the master gradually fell under the power of drink and began to abuse his animals. When one night he came home drunk and grabbed the cat, Pluto bit him and in a fit of rage he blinded the cat in one eye with his penknife. Some months later he went further and hanged his beloved pet from a tree in the garden. However, that same night his house caught fire and he, his wife and their servant only just managed to escape in time. The following morning a crowd gathered around the only wall left standing — the one against which his bed rested — and were amazed to see that the body of the hanged cat, complete with the rope around its neck, had somehow been flattened onto the plaster above the bedhead.

The man was very worried about all this and decided to look for another cat to replace the murdered one. One evening, whilst drinking, he noticed a large black cat with a white bib sitting in the bar and, as it seemed very friendly and no one appeared to own it, he took it home. But, when he noticed that it too had only one eye he began to dislike it. But the more he hated the cat the more it pestered him and as time progressed the white patch on its fur grew larger and larger and began to take the distinct shape of a gallows.

Unable to stand the constant attentions of the now loathsome creature, the man eventually took an axe to it but when his wife interposed herself he killed her instead and decided to wall up the body in the cellar. Three days passed and, though suspicions were aroused, no evidence of the murder was found. In addition, there was no sign of the cat and the man began to rest easy. However, on the fourth day the police arrived and thoroughly searched the place and were just about to leave when the man, proud of his workmanship, tapped the wall where his wife was buried to show the soundness of the building. Just at that moment a hideous wail emerged from behind the wall, growing in intensity. The police immediately chipped

off the plaster to reveal the body of the man's wife, standing upright with the cat sitting on her broken head — he had buried the cat with his wife!

Grippeminault, Archduke of the Furrycats

Grippeminault, or **Clawpuss** as his name is sometimes translated, is the fearsome judge in Rabelais' *Gargantua and Pantagruel*. Pantagruel and his band of adventurers have just sailed past the islands of Procreation and Condemnation and landed on the shores of the Wicket when they are arrested by a group of Furrycats. These, we are told, are a hideous race whose fur grows inwards and who feed on little children and marble stones. They have long, steel-tipped claws, wear caps or mortarboards on their heads, and strange pouches are slung about their bodies. They live entirely on plunder and kill anything that crosses their path, with no sense of good or evil. A beggar tries to warn the travellers of their danger as they approach the courtroom but it is too late, their exit has been blocked and the only way out is to answer a riddle propounded by Grippeminault. Their first sight of the mighty judge is truly frightening. Surrounded by thunderbolts he has three heads in one — a roaring lion, a fawning dog and a ravening wolf — interlaced with a dragon biting its own tail. His bloody hands have harpies' claws, and he has tusks like a four-year-old boar, eyes 'like hell's throat' and is entirely covered in pestles and mortars.

At first the miserable prisoners are completely stumped by the riddle but when Panurge's turn comes he solves it immediately and throws a bag of gold crowns into the centre of the court. At this they are released and after a few minor skirmishes near the harbour, make good their escape. (**Rabelais, François, Gargantua, Pantagruel, Panurge**)

Lillian, the speakeasy cat

In Damon Runyon's story of the same name, **Lillian** is a scrawny little black kitten which the drunken cabaret crooner Wilbur Willard finds on the sidewalk one cold snowy morning in New York in the 1940s. Believing her to be a leopard he pockets the kitten and takes her home to his top-floor apartment in the flophouse Hotel de Brussels. He names the cat after his former partner whose departure in the arms of a richer man broke up their song-and-dance vaudeville act and reduced Wilbur to his present miserable state. However, with the arrival of the cat he perks up considerably and he and the little creature are constant companions, the cat becoming a familiar sight around Broadway as it trots beside him or sits on his shoulder. As she fattens up Lillian becomes more self-confident and is soon terrorizing the local lapdogs, and very nearly gets Wilbur into a brawl when she drags a Pekinese home by the scruff of its neck, hotly pursued by its owner and her bootlegger husband. She also starts making friends in the neighbourhood and is soon very fond of the little boy who lives across the passage in the hotel.

Early one morning Wilbur staggers into Mindy's bar alone, having had a few at Good Time Charley's speakeasy (Charley doesn't admit cats), when a man bursts in with the news that the Hôtel de Brussels is on fire. Bemused rather than alarmed, Wilbur staggers off to watch the flames and is so delighted that he goes into the blazing inferno to fetch Lillian to watch it too.

Miraculously he reappears shortly afterwards carrying the cat, who claws him and leaps back into the hotel. To the crowd's amazement he then enters the flames once more and is later seen on the roof carrying the cat and the neighbour's small boy. After leaping into the firemen's safety net he tells the narrator that the second time he went in he saw the by now

smouldering cat sniffing at some liquid under a door and pushed the door in to get a blanket to wrap her up in. When he pulled a blanket off the nearest bed he happened to see the boy and grabbed him too — a man lying sprawled on the floor grasping a bottle was obviously dead so he left him there.

The press and the boy's mother were naturally ecstatic about the heroic rescue and when Wilbur appears again some years later it emerges that his valour had somehow attracted back his old flame, they had married and Wilbur was now very prosperous. However, it is only now that the true story of the cat in the burning hotel is revealed.

Apparently, because he didn't like to drink alone, Wilbur used to lace Lillian's milk with whisky and after a while the cat too became a 'rumpot' — which explained the vicious attacks on the poodles etc. when she'd had a few. Also, it just so happened that the hotel fire took place at about the time that Wilbur normally came home to give her her tipple, and when he took her out the first time without her toddy she immediately raced back indoors and found the whisky seeping out from the dead man's bottle — it was this she was sniffing under the door! Asked what the old soak was doing now, Wilbur said that she had moved in with the bootlegger whose wife owned the Peke she had nearly killed and was in her element drinking booze and whacking the long-suffering hound from time to time. (**Damon**, **Wilbur**, **Willard**, **Broadway**, **Mindy**, **Rumpot**, **Tipples**)

A cat fable

In the tale of 'The Cat that Walked by Himself' in Kipling's *Just So Stories,* Man manages to persuade the dog, the horse and the cow to give up their freedom in return for food and protection. The cat, however, will have none of this and makes a separate special arrangement with Woman. In return for a regular supply of milk and a guaranteed place by the hearth he

will catch mice and be kind to babies but otherwise be free to do as he pleases. When he has performed his duties '...he is the cat that walks by himself...Then he goes out to the Wet Wild Woods...waving his wild tail and walking by his wild lone.' (**Wildwood**, *Solo*, **Kipling**)

A self-help manual for cats

The typescript of *The Silent Miaow*, a handbook for kittens, strays and homeless cats, was supposedly deposited on the doorstep of a publisher neighbour of Paul Gallico's in West-hampton, Long Island one day. As it appeared to be typed in some sort of code he gave it to Gallico who had had experience of cryptoanalysis during the war years. However, after closer examination he discovered that the script was in fact typed in English but had been repeatedly mis-keyed, and when the contents were revealed it was obvious that this was done by a paw print on a very sensitive electric typewriter. The first sentence read: 'When I wad z vety ypung koteb 9 jad tje mosfortine ti lise mt motjer abd fymd mys4lf akone 9n tje wolrf zt aye if s9x w44ks' ('When I was a very young kitten I had the misfortune to lose my mother and find myself alone in the world at the age of six weeks').

After carefully piecing together the narrative behind the manual's instructions — which detail how to 'take over' a house, with tips on men, women, children, food, vets, doors, motherhood etc. — and making enquiries amongst the locals, it appeared that the most likely culprit was **Cica**, a tabby-and-white cat owned by the Schorr family. Using what remained of the supplied text (the cat author's name had been obliterated and the conclusion was incomplete) and incorporating photo-graphs of Cica's upbringing, Gallico then 'edited' the com-plete book for publication, keeping the US spellings as it was an American cat. The publisher, himself a confirmed cat-hater, hoped that despite being the greatest literary find since

The Young Visiters the book would expose the wiles of the manipulative cat. But this proved in vain, as the public admired her ingenuity all the more.

The title of the work comes from the strange soundless cry described by the feline author as being irresistible to humans and which thus can be used as the cat's ultimate secret weapon in the take-over battle.

Belling the cat

The practice of 'belling the cat' first finds its place in English literature in the prologue to William Langland's 14th-century allegorical poem, *Piers Plowman*. Here a rat suggests that one method of surviving the attacks of a marauding cat might be to fix a bell round its neck so that they can hear its approach. All the assembled rodents think this is a good idea and a collar with bells is brought, but no one wants to have the task of attaching it to the cat's neck. A mouse then speaks up gloomily and says that even if they managed to get rid of this cat another one, or its kitten, would take its place. This was seen as a clear allusion to the situation in England at the time, with the rats and mice being the harassed commoners and Edward III the tyrannical cat. His 'kitten' was his grandson and heir Richard. (**Piers**)

Cat bards

Many owners have waxed lyrical about their pets and to some their cat is pure poetry in motion. But for verse of a more static, if no less devotional kind we must look to the professionals themselves. The French poet Baudelaire was dotty about cats and, as well as including three items dedicated to them in his *Les Fleurs Du Mal* collection, apparently used to cause considerably embarrassment whenever he visited people — on whatever business — by first seeking out the household pet, picking it up and kissing and fondling it. As he was also a

well-known alcoholic perhaps absinthe made the bard grow fonder!

An 8th-century Irish manuscript featuring the exploits of a heroic white cat called **Pangur Ban** exists but perhaps the earliest mention of a cat in a poem is that by the 6th-century Greek epigrammatist Agathias, who heaped opprobrium on the murderer of his pet partridge. The first published verses in praise of a cat were those to **Belaud** by the French 16th-century writer Joachim du Bellay, though Tasso's sonnets to his cat can't be far behind. In the same century, by contrast, John Skelton vilified 'Gyb, our cat savage...of churlyshe kynde' for destroying poor Phylyp Sparowe in his long poem. And later it is the splendid Persian **Atossa** which features in Matthew Arnold's well-known verses to Matthias.

But many others have sung the cat's praises, from minor works by Keats, Wordsworth and Shelley, through Christina Rossetti, Cowper and Swinburne to Yeats's **Minnaloushe**, the three black cats in De la Mare's 'Five Eyes', various works by W.H. Davies, Bret Harte and Ella Wheeler Wilcox and the doleful laments of Gray's ode to Selima and Thomas Hardy's sad lines on the death of his cat. And of course, the writings of the Old Possum himself, T.S. Eliot. (*Baudelaire*, *Agathias*, *Joachim*, *Bellay*, *Tasso*, *Bret*, *Ella*, *Hardy*, *Possum*, *Matthias*)

Sylvia, the society cat

First published in 1954, Sandy Wilson's *This is Sylvia* purports to be the memoirs of a classy Persian now happily married and living in Surrey with her three kittens from a previous liaison. The daughter of an aristocratic Persian and a bohemian tabby with a ginger streak, **Sylvia** takes to the stage when her mother leaves for California with millionaire whiting-cannery boss **Cyrus T. Rocksalmonfeller**, modelling for *Chatte* magazine in her spare time. By a series of lucky breaks she rockets to stardom, tours the USA, is reunited with her mother and finds her way into the movies. In Hollywood she runs off with **Blackie Diabolo**, the suave halibut-oil magnate and lover of glamour-queen **Miaow-Miaow Latouche**. To escape the scandal they decamp to Nice but the jilted Ms Latouche cattily gets her revenge by exposing Diabolo as a complete fraud and he is arrested. Sylvia then becomes a nun in Florence before moving into the villa of a writer friend of her mentor and guardian, Hester Briggs. Here she meets her future husband **Sir Algernon Gutts-Whytyng**. They become better acquainted on Sylvia's return to London and their marriage is the Wedding of the Year. However, when their children turn out to be less than pure Persian and Sir Algernon is later photographed with another cat at the Pussyfoot Club, Sylvia realizes it's all over, sues for divorce and moves in with **Lucy**, an old girlfriend. It is whilst she is entertaining some of Lucy's political friends that she meets the City businessman who becomes her second and, she hopes, final husband.

Tobermory, the talking cat

In Saki's short story 'Tobermory' the setting is Sir Wilfrid and Lady Blemley's house party on a rainy afternoon in August. Among the guests is Cornelius Appin who, after 17 years' research, claims to have discovered the means for instructing animals in the art of human speech and that in the last few months the Blemleys' own cat, **Tobermory**, has become his first successful pupil.

The other guests and indeed the hosts themselves are very sceptical about this and suspect some kind of ventriloquist act, but when Sir Wilfrid departs in search of the sleeping cat and receives the reply that he'll come when he feels like it, in a very off-hand human voice, the company is stunned. Later Tobermory strolls in, casually accepts milk and in a bored and condescending tone replies to the rather trivial questions put to him by the humans. However, when he begins to reveal personal

comments made by both guests and hosts about each other behind their backs the situation becomes rather embarrassing. To change the subject the Major alludes to Tobermory's philandering with a tortoiseshell in the stables but is cut short when the cat counters with remarks about the Major's own amorous affairs. Luckily for all present the conversation is then interrupted as Tobermory flashes out into the garden in pursuit of a large yellow tom seen heading for the stables.

At this point, after some discussion, the members of the party are agreed that rather than risk exposure of their private lives to all and sundry, Tobermory should be poisoned forthwith and, despite Appin's protestations at the destruction of his life's work, a strychnine-laced dish of fish scraps is left out for the cat. When Tobermory fails to reappear they fear the worst but are greatly relieved when his body is found in the shrubbery next morning, apparently the victim of the large yellow tom. The danger now over, the guests depart and some time later a news report reveals that Appin has been killed trying to teach German irregular verbs to an elephant in Dresden Zoo. (**Wilfrid, Cornelius**)

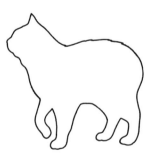

MARMALADES, STRIPES AND TABBIES

Agneatha/Gemma/Muppet — Tabbies owned by cat-painter Lesley Anne Ivory. (Also *Minouche*, *Octopussy*, *Peepo* and *Ruskin*.)

Atabis/Attabiah — (See *Weird, Wild and Wonderful Cats*.)

Baby-Puss — After the sabre-tooth tiger that features as Fred and Wilma's pet and locks Fred out in the closing credits of Hanna-Barbera's *The Flintstones* animated TV series about two Stone Age families, the Flintstones and the Rubbles. (*Wilma, Hanna*)

Barre-en-Rouille — A big red-and-black-striped cat owned by the French novelist J. K. Huysmans (see *Cats of the Famous*).

Bee — For a striped black-and-orange cat.

Belle — (See *Exotics and Rare Breeds*.)

Brindle — For a brown- or grey-streaked cat.

Bumble — For a black-and-yellow/orange bumblebee-like cat.

Chivers — A marmalade cat.

Cica — After the tabby-and-white cat that allegedly wrote *The Silent Miaow* (see *Fictional Cats*).

Cooper — A superior (Oxford) marmalade. (*Oxford*)

Cupid — (See *Exotics and Rare Breeds*.)

Deborah — For a black-and-orange furball, after the Hebrew word meaning 'a bee'.

Dusty — (See *Record-Breaking Cats*.)

Emma/Emily — A perfect name for tabby cats that have an 'M' pattern in the fur on their foreheads. And indeed doubly appropriate in the case of the latter name as all the Brontë sisters, but particularly Emily, adored cats. (*Brontë*)

Faith — After the brave tabby female who lived near St Paul's Cathedral during the Blitz and was awarded a medal for courage (see *Top Cats*).

Fawn — For a light-brown cat, especially one that is overly fond and fawning.

Fritz — The film *Fritz the Cat* (1972), based on Robert Crumb's bawdy, brawling, collar-and-tie-wearing marmalade tom and his seedy New York streetwise friends, was the first-ever X-rated animated cartoon, largely for eroticism, violence and strong language (see *Comical Cats*). (*Robert*, *Crumb*)

Garfield — Love him or loathe him, this heavy-lidded pasta-chomping, smart Alec, striped ginger cat was created by Jim Davis in 1977 and is currently one of the most popular cartoon characters ever. (See *Comical Cats*.)

Gus/Asparagus — T. S. Eliot's theatre cat who once played a tiger.

Heathcliff — Now a major TV series, the clever marmalade tom Heathcliff, with his elderly owners and pretty Persian friend **Sonja**, were first produced by George Gatley for McNaught Syndicate in 1973 as a newspaper panel — perhaps too for a cat that likes the moors?

Himmy — A monstrous Australian tabby that holds the world heavyweight record for a cat (see *Record-Breaking Cats*).

Hornet — For a vicious striped cat that objects to being disturbed.

Jazz — After the only animal passenger aboard the airship R-34 (see *Record-Breaking Cats*), or for any hot dude or cool cat.

Jennyanydots — After T. S. Eliot's Old **Gumbie** cat who sits and sits.

Ma — After the oldest cat on record, a female tabby from Devon (see *Record-Breaking Cats*).

Marmaduke — A perfect name for a marmalade cat but also after the famous Marmaduke **Gingerbits** who became the subject of a long tug-of-love legal battle that filled the British newspapers in 1984.

Maxim — For a red-and-gold cat, after the décor of the famous Paris restaurant.

Melampyge — A tabby cat that used to inhabit the Campanile in Venice's St Mark's Square.

Minnie — A famous rat-catching tabby of this name lived in London's White City stadium (see *Top Cats*).

O'Malley/Duchess — After the singing alleycat in Walt Disney's *The Aristocats* (1970), who rescues the refined Parisian cat Duchess and her three kittens when they are abducted and dumped in the French countryside (see *Comical Cats*). Duchess was also the name of a cat owned by the painter Wilson Steer. (**Wilson**)

Orlando — After the marmalade cat in the stories by Kathleen Hale and the ginger-and-white resident of London's Chelsea Arts Club. (**Kathleen**)

Papillon — A good name for a tabby with the authentic butterfly pattern over its shoulders (*papillon* is French for 'butterfly').

Rajah — (See *Exotics and Rare Breeds*.)

Riff-Raff — Star of *Cats & Co,* a TV cartoon series created by Jean Chalopin and Bruno Bianchi, Riff-Raff is a yellow-ginger US alleycat tom who wears a cap and a scarf and, like his more famous predecessor, Top Cat, leads his own gang.

Ruffie — (See *Exotics and Rare Breeds.*)

Rumpelstilzchen — Rumpelstiltskin was the German fairytale dwarf whose name the King's bride had to guess or lose her first child; it was also one of many names given to a remarkable cat owned by the poet Robert Southey (see *Cats of the Famous*).

Rybolov — Meaning 'fisherman', this was one of the classical composer Borodin's cats, a male tabby so named because it used to break holes in the ice and catch fish through them with its paws (see *Weird, Wild and Wonderful Cats*).

Selima — Selima was Horace Walpole's adored tabby which was drowned in a goldfish bowl and immortalized in a poem by Gray (see *Cats of the Famous*).

Shere Khan -- Shere Khan was Mowgli's enemy in Kipling's *The Jungle Book*, later made into a Disney cartoon. A lame tiger, he repeatedly tried to attack the boy but eventually was trampled to death by a herd of cattle sent by Mowgli.

Tabitha — After Mrs Tabitha Twitchit in the stories by Beatrix Potter.

Tammany — The Tammany Tiger was a cartoon representation of William 'Boss' Tweed's corrupt Tammany Hall organization in New York City. Drawn by Thomas Nast, the anti-Tweed cartoon campaign successfully prevented the Democrats being returned to power in the city and

Tweed himself was eventually imprisoned.

Tango — After a marmalade tom owned by Winston Churchill and painted by Sir William Nicholson (see *Cats of the Famous*).

Thomson — The tee-shirt-wearing marmalade cartoon cat with white paws and a white-tipped tail that appears on TV and elsewhere in the UK advertising Thomson Directories' range of local classified telephone directories.

Tiddles — A famous railway cat who was master of the ladies' loo on Platform 1 at London's Paddington Station (see *Top Cats*). (**Paddington**)

Tigger — Tigger was the 'large and helpful' tiger in A.A. Milne's *The House at Pooh Corner* and was a very bouncy animal 'with a way of saying How-do-you-do which always left your ears full of sand'. For a very bouncy cat.

Tippy — The British record-holder for being the most prolific mother cat is Tippy the tabby from Kingston upon Hull, who produced 343 kittens.

Tony — Tony is the cartoon tiger wearing a kerchief that appears on packets of Kellogg's Frosties breakfast cereal and in TV advertisements, declaring that they are 'G-r-r-r-reat!'

Torquata — This is the description of a classical tabby with narrow vertical stripes — not to be confused with Torquemada, the first chief of the Spanish Inquisition, though many a tabby has tortured its prey... (*Torquemada*)

Twiglet — Another of Lesley Anne Ivory's cats, but also a good name for a marmalade-striped cat, after the Marmite-flavoured snack sticks.

TOP CATS

Slippers, the White House cat

When Theodore Roosevelt was President of the United States the unquestioned master of the White House was his six-toed grey cat, **Slippers** — so-named because of his larger than usual feet. Whenever a diplomatic dinner or summit conference was held Slippers would make sure he was always the centre of attention, to such a degree that on one occasion in 1906 he even blocked the access to a banquet by sprawling across a rug in the entrance — the President, his aides and international ambassadors from every corner of the globe had to walk around him!

Frequently absent for days and even weeks on end, Slippers had remarkable prescient powers and always returned home when a high-level meeting was imminent. Indeed, so reliable a guide were his movements to the goings-on at the White House that journalists would eagerly await the cat's reappearance in the grounds as a harbinger of major events. (*Theodore*)

Mysouff, the telepathic cat

Alexandre Dumas *père*, author of *The Three Musketeers* etc., had amongst his many pets a cat called **Mysouff** which also possessed what can only be described as telepathic powers.

When living with his mother in Paris, Dumas worked as a clerk to the Duke of Orléans. Each day he would set off for his office regularly at 9.30 a.m, returning at 5.30 p.m. And every morning the faithful cat would accompany his master part of the way and be waiting at the same spot to 'collect' him in the evening. However, if for some reason Dumas was held up at the office the cat always seemed to know and no amount of coaxing would make him leave his favourite cushion by the fireside. Conversely, if by some oversight the cat was accidentally shut in when his master was due home he would scratch furiously to be let out.

The telepathic cat's successor, **Mysouff II**, a black-and-white foundling, had none of his namesake's talents and indeed appears to have been a less reliable pet all round. One day, with the help of three of the family's tame monkeys, he broke into Dumas's aviary and ate all his rare and valuable exotic birds. Once captured the culprits were solemnly 'tried' by Dumas and his friends and sentenced to five years' imprisonment in the birds' cage! (*Alex, Alexandre*)

Towser, the mouser

It must be tough being a mouse in Scotland. For in the shadows behind the barrels in the Glenturret whisky distillery near Crieff in Perthshire there once lurked a real dragon of a cat — the world's champion mouser, an ace amongst aces. A pretty tortoiseshell female to her human friends, **Towser** was the terror of the Macmice and averaged three kills a day despite (or perhaps because of!) the alcohol-heavy fumes of the premises. In total she despatched over 25,000 of the little rodents.

And when it comes to the larger variety, London's White City was not a place to tarry in the first half of this century, for here reigned a voracious tabby by the name of **Minnie**. Between 1927 and 1933 she pushed no less than 12,480 rats down the celestial drain — a record that still stands today.

Simon, the heroic cat VC

Surely one of the bravest cats of all time must be the black-and-white neutered male mascot of the frigate HMS *Amethyst*, which was awarded a posthumous Dickin Medal — the pet's VC (and the only one awarded to a cat) — for his heroic actions during the Yangtse Incident in 1949.

As a kitten in May of the previous year, the handsome **Simon** had first boarded the ship when presented to its captain, Lieutenant-Commander I.R. Griffiths, then stationed in Hong Kong. His cheery nature and natural aptitude for rounding up and destroying all manner of vermin on the ship quickly endeared him to the crew, who treated him as a respected member of the ship's company.

So when the Chinese Communist Army began to threaten British interests on the Yangtse River near Nanking, it was perfectly natural that when the frigate was despatched to the battlezone its white-pawed mascot should accompany them. However, as the *Amethyst* approached Nanking it came under heavy bombardment from the Communist shore-batteries and, badly crippled, ran aground — many of the crew being killed or injured.

During the attack Simon had been in the captain's cabin as a guest at his dinner table but was thrown across the room when a shell burst inside, killing the commander instantly. However, though badly burnt and injured by flying shrapnel, Simon soon recovered himself sufficiently to notice that a number of rats had been disturbed by the battle and were now roaming the ship, threatening the health of every member of the crew. Despite his wounds, the brave cat immediately went on the attack and whilst still under heavy fire repeatedly chased and caught the disease-carrying rodents.

When, finally, the acting commander of the *Amethyst* led the limping frigate into Hong Kong harbour — after a miraculous

168-mile moonlit dash — Simon's fame had preceded him and well-wishers crowded round to marvel at the heroic mascot. However, Simon's enjoyment of his hour of glory was short-lived as his health had been seriously undermined by the battle and he eventually succumbed to his wounds whilst in quarantine on 28 November 1949.

In a grand ceremony on 13 April of the following year, the Lord Mayor of Plymouth posthumously awarded Simon the Dickin Medal for 'meritorious and distinguished service'. The citation read: 'Served on HMS *Amethyst* during the Yangtse Incident, disposing of many rats though wounded by shellblast. Throughout this incident his behaviour was of the highest order, although the blast was capable of making a hole over a foot in diameter in steel-plate.'

Simon was buried with full honours in the PDSA cemetery in Ilford, Essex, where a specially carved headstone now commemorates this most heroic of cats. (**Dickin**, **Griff**, **Griffiths**, **Amethyst**, **Yangtse**)

A cat senator

To prove that students paid little attention to whom they voted for, Diane E. Oltman entered her cat as a candidate for election to the Student Senate of Southern Illinois University in September 1971. The cat, **D.E. Gordon Oltman**, won the majority of the votes — on the platform of the problem of stray dogs on the campus — and was duly elected to the Senate. Though whether Ms Oltman felt her point was thereby proven is not recorded...(**Diane**)

Ginger, a cat Einstein

One of the curiosities of the Patent Office in London is an item lodged by Arthur Pedwick of Selsey, Sussex, in March 1976 for a 'chromatic cat-flap control unit' which would allow his ginger cat into the house but not the neighbour's **Blackie**.

As the patent specification records, when Mr Pedwick showed the plans of the radiation-detecting device to **Ginger** he was pleasantly surprised when the cat pointed out a further use for the invention as a nuclear deterrent. If all the nations of the world agreed to launch a 1,000-megaton Complete Nuclear Disintegration (CND) bomb into orbit with his device attached, it could be programmed to fall on whichever country originated a nuclear attack on another. Thus, fear of this automatic independent reprisal system would deter all as it would be suicide to make a first strike. One might say it was the purrfect solution. (*Selsey*)

The Tower of London cat

The family records of the Wyat (or Wyatt) family tell a remarkable story of cat charity that saved the life of Sir Henry Wyat (1460-1537), who survived to become a major English statesman of the 16th century and to sire the illustrious diplomat and poet, Sir Thomas Wyat (1503-42).

An outspoken adherent of the Lancastrian party in politics as a young man, Henry rapidly fell out of favour with Richard III and was incarcerated in the forbidding Tower of London, where he was denied all food and repeatedly tortured. In the circumstances, death would have been inevitable in a matter of weeks, if not days, under these conditions but for the appearance at regular intervals of a cat in Wyat's cell. The records neither name this feline angel of mercy nor describe its appearance or how it got past the guards, but that it managed to supply the starving Wyat with a number of pigeons to eat is well documented.

Thanks to the cat's good offices, Wyat survived long enough to witness the accession of Henry VII, after which he was released and quickly recovered his health. When Henry VIII succeeded his father in 1509, Wyat became Knight of the Bath, knight banneret, and held various offices at court. His more

famous son, Thomas, was also knighted and also imprisoned in the Tower — on one occasion to prevent him marrying Anne Boleyn whom Henry had taken a fancy to — but only for short periods, so the Tower cat's services were not required again. However, it is certain that without the help of this anonymous feline benefactor England would have lost not just one but two of its finest diplomats and an important Renaissance poet (Thomas was not conceived until Henry had been released from prison). (**Wyat, Wyatt**)

Faith of St Paul's

Faith was a brave little tabby cat who lived with the rector of St Augustus's church near St Paul's in London. During the Blitz in World War II when German bombs rained down and devastated the surrounding area, Faith carried her black-and-white kitten **Panda** down into the basement of the rectory and on 9 September 1940 when the building received a direct hit, protected her charge from the falling debris, explosions and fire. The following day both cats were found safe beneath the rubble and in recognition of her 'steadfast courage in the Battle of London' Faith was awarded a specially struck medal from the PDSA as, being a 'civilian' cat, she did not qualify for the Dickin Medal, the animals' VC.

Tiddles, the railway cat

One of the most famous — and fattest! — British cats was **Tiddles** of Paddington Station, London, whose celebrity in his lifetime far outshone that of the station's mascot, Paddington Bear.

Master of the ladies' loo on Platform 1, this delightful tom padded his way where all men fear to tread and ruled supreme for 13 years. He first appeared in 1970 as a tiny six-week-old kitten — a silver-grey tabby with white paws and bib — and was immediately adopted by the lavatory's attendant, Mrs June

Watson. From then on his reputation began to grow, as did his girth — a daily diet that could include chicken livers, lambs' tongues, kidneys, rabbit or steak pushed his bulk up to a maximum 32lb (14.5kg) — and in 1982 he became London Fat Cat Champion.

The exotic food brought by admirers was stored in Tiddles's personal fridge, his basket was like a throne and fan mail arrived regularly from all over the world. He was filmed by both New Zealand and Canadian camera crews and his international press-cuttings filled two scrapbooks. And such was his adopted owner's devotion to Tiddles that when she was offered early retirement after 42 years of service with British Rail she turned it down rather than take him away from 'home' in the station.

Tiddles died as he had lived, in a blaze of publicity, on 2 November 1983. Ironically for a railway cat, he used to hate the sound of high-speed trains. (*Paddington, June*)

A popular party puss

700 cats attended the 23rd birthday of **Tommy Clark**, a yellow tomcat living in Seneca Falls, New York, in the late 1930s, and the following year no less than 1,500 guests were invited from all over the USA, including President Roosevelt (who unfortunately was unable to attend). An honorary member of the Benevolent and Protective Order of Elks, Master Clark always wore the emblem of the lodge on a red ribbon around his neck on these ceremonial occasions.

'Carry On' cat that missed the boat

In February 1939 the *Manchester Evening Chronicle* reported the remarkable adventure of **Sidney James**, a ship's cat working on a meat boat (nice work if you can get it ...). As was his wont, Sidney went ashore when the ship docked at Bootle but, despite repeated sounding of the klaxon, he failed to return in time for sailing and the crew waved goodbye to the cat left on

the dockside as they headed off on their 5000-mile voyage to South America. When the steamer pulled into the harbour at Buenos Aires, however, to their utter amazement the sailors found Master James quietly sitting on the quayside awaiting their arrival! Miaowing a welcome to his old shipmates, he purposefully strode up the gangplank ahead of customs officials before settling down in his favourite spot as if nothing had happened. It turned out that he had caught the faster mail boat which had left the same night as his own ship but arrived six days earlier. What a carry on!

A wondrous cat

Saki's story of Tobermory the talking cat seems only possible in fiction yet, amazing to relate, a *real* talking cat was exhibited at the Circus Busch in Berlin in 1927. Named **Peter Alupka** the Wonder Cat, its owner, Dr Sutoris, had taught him to cry out various names such as 'Anna' and 'Helen', accompany his wife in the song 'Der Mai ist Gekommen' and round off the whole act with three cheers of 'Hurrah'! Peter Alupka caused a sensation when he first appeared and such was his fame that a gramophone record was made of his performance. (*Sutoris*)

Tiger in the house

When General and Mrs Price put their Chelsea house up for sale they decided to leave their cat **Tiger** behind in the home to which he was accustomed. However, though a number of prospective buyers came to view the property in fashionable Eaton Terrace, none would take on the forlorn-looking tailless tabby, even as a gift. Determined to move at all costs, the Prices reluctantly agreed that if an offer hadn't been made within a fortnight they would kill the cat. As the days ticked by, Tiger was well fed and cared for, little knowing that his nine lives were fast running out. Then, only two days before the appointed date of his execution a friend of the family rang to say

that he'd overheard the clerk of the House of Lords saying that he was looking for a mouser. Tiger was duly despatched to the Mother of Parliaments and, despite initial disapproval by some peers at his deficiency in the tail department, was taken on in the autumn of 1939. He quickly vindicated himself by catching two mice that very same day. However, when later General and Mrs Price came to visit their former pet, having obtained a special pass to enter the House, Tiger, quite understandably, refused to acknowledge them.

TORTOISESHELLS, PARTICOLOURS AND MONGRELS

Allerleirauh — The girl who has a coat made of 1,000 skins in the Grimms' fairytale (also called 'Cat-skin').

Amalgam — A mixture.

Bayadère — After the fabric with horizontal stripes.

Bedlam — A chaotic jumble.

Bike — For a bicolour type.

Bitz/Bitsy — A bits-and-pieces cat.

Bunch — A disparate handful.

Bundle — All sorts fused together.

Calico — Another name for 'tortoiseshell'.

Cappriciosa — After the chef's 'special' variety pizza (from the Italian for 'capricious').

Carnival — For a garishly coloured, festive cat. Also, as 'carnival' means 'meat farewell' perhaps for one that prefers fish?

Chintz — An old name for a tortoiseshell-and-white cat.

Chowder — A good name for a mongrel, after the clam or fish stew.

Chroma — Greek for 'colour'.

Chutney — (See 'Pickles'.)

Cloaks — Or perhaps a good name might be **Wardrobe**, where lots of coats are hung together?

Clobber — Slang for clothes and perhaps also for a violent cat?

Clump — A group of almost anything.

Cockade — A tricolour, red, white and blue cat.

Cocktail — A heady mixture.

Confetti — For a festive feline all different hues.

Dapple — For any mixed-colour type, but also for a grey with darker spots.

Dolly — A Dolly Mixture cat.

Doodles — The colours go all over the place.

Farrago — From the Latin for 'mixture'.

Flex — For a supple cat whose fur is covered in coloured flecks.

Flicker — A kaleidoscope-coated kitty.

Galaxy — Who can count its constituents?

Gallico — Gallico the calico cat — after cat writer Paul Gallico.

Gallimaufry — Another word for a hotch-potch.

Gaudy — For a cat that's ablaze with colour.

Gobelin — After the exquisite French tapestries.

Goulash — A paprika-flavoured Hungarian stew so perhaps for a 'hungry' cat with dark red predominating?

Gumbo/Gombo — A stew.

Harlequin — A cat with multicoloured diamond patterns and a black face or mask.

Hartley — For a jammy puss. Also after Hartley Coleridge who wrote a poem about his cat. (*Coleridge*)

Hotch-potch — One that looks like meat and vegetable stew, or any mess of pottage.

Hughes/Huey — A cat of many hues.

Imbroglio — Confusion reigns.

Iris — Iris was the goddess of the rainbow — for a cat that's a crock of gold.

Jacob — For a cat with a Coat of Many Colours.

Josephine — The cat in Patrick Chalmers's poem 'The Tortoiseshell Cat'.

Jumble/Jumbly — A good mongrel name.

Kaleidoscope — From the Greek meaning 'beautiful form' — a doubly good name for a pretty, variegated type.

Kimono — Another name for the Japanese Bobtail cat, after the long garment. (See *Weird, Wild and Wonderful Cats*.)

Kingfisher — For an ace angler puss, perhaps also one dressed in the colours of this bird: blue, orange and white. (*Halcyon*)

Maneki — A Maneki-Neko is a tricolour Japanese pottery good-luck cat (see *Cats in the Arts*).

Marbles — For a streaky, marbled white, black or grey cat, or perhaps one with glass-ball-like eyes. Alternatively for a highly intelligent cat that certainly hasn't lost his marbles!

Mayhem — For a mixed-up, maddening cat.

Medley — A various puss.

Mélange — French for 'mixture'.

Mi-Ke — The name for the Japanese Bobtail cat with a black, red and white coat, but an Anglicized one wouldn't mind being called **Mike**.

Misto — Italian for 'mixture'.

Motley — The particoloured attire of a jester...

Mourka — A white-and-ginger dancing cat owned by choreographer George Balanchine (see *Cats in the Arts*). Mourka was also a heroic cat who featured in the Battle of Stalingrad, described by *The Times* on 13 January 1943 as carrying messages about enemy gun-emplacements to Russians besieged by the Germans in the city. (*Balanchine*)

Muddles — For a mongrel.

Mufti — A cat that can't find his uniform coat?

Neapolitan — After the Naples ice-cream that has layers of differing colours, for a cool cat.

Oddbod/Oddments/Oddjob — A mongrel.

Paraphernalia — A bunch of miscellaneous bits.

Pasticcio — A work of art in many styles...

Peregrine — After Peregrine Pickle in Smollett's book (and see 'Pickles'). The name also means 'wanderer'.

Pickles — A cat that not only looks like a mixture of everything but constantly seems to be in a pickle. And after a female kitten described by Leigh Hunt.

Pizza — For a cat that's pizza this and pizza that?

Polly — After the tortoiseshell kitten with white paws owned by children's writer and founder of Puffin Books, Kaye Webb — a good name for a polychrome cat. (*Kaye*)

Popinjay — A brightly coloured cat.

Pot Pourri — For a pot purr-i puss!

Ragamuffin/Rags/Ragbag — A scruffy mongrel of assorted colours.

Ragoût/Ratatouille — Two types of French stew, for a 'French' or long-haired variety.

Rainbow — A brilliantly hued cat that always appears after the rain?

Renoir — An Impressionist work of art?

Salad — A healthy mixture.

Salami/Mortadella/Sausages — Who knows what goes into them...

Sandwich — Almost any colours squeezed between white or brown.

Scraps — Odds and ends, for a this-and-that cat.

Scrubs — A tatty mongrel.

Smitty — After one of the oldest cats to have given birth, a tortoiseshell who produced her first kitten at the age of 28 in 1953.

Sophocles — The great playwright is reputed to have met his end when a passing bird, thinking his bald pate was a shining rock, dropped a tortoise it was carrying on to his head to break the shell open! For a tortoiseshell cat?

Spangles — After the boiled sweets, each one a different colour.

Spatters — What a carelessly handled paintbrush does...

Spectrum — The whole range...

Stew — For a mixture cat that is best when simmered down.

Ticky — Ticking is having up to three bands of contrasting colour on each hair of fur, as in Abyssinian cats. Ticky was also the eponymous soldier hero of Stella Gibbons's comic novel, so perhaps for a multicoloured cat with a military bearing. (*Stella*)

Topsy — A prizewinning 19th-century Tortoiseshell Chinchilla, but a good name for any cat (if you have two why not call the other **Turvy**?).

Tortie — For a tortoiseshell.

Towser — After a Scottish tortoiseshell which holds the world record for catching mice (see *Top Cats*).

Trifle — A fruity cat with white and yellow predominating — and for one not to be trifled with!

Tutti-Frutti — A complete mish-mash of colours.

Vair — The heraldic term for a kind of variegated fur.

SCREEN CATS

A double Oscar cat

The Picture Animal Top Star of the Year (PATSY) awards were inaugurated in 1951 by the American Humane Association and many of these animal Oscars have been won by cats. The most successful feline film star to date is **Orangey** who has walked off with no less than two Patsys for his purrfect performances, including the first one ever awarded to a cat.

In his first award-winning role, as the eponymous hero of *Rhubarb* (1951), Orangey played the owner of a baseball team called the New York Loons. However, apparently there was a slight contretemps during shooting between Orangey and one of the co-stars — a certain Ray Milland — and the matter was only resolved with some difficulty when Milland's hands were smeared with liver paste and catnip in an attempt to get Orangey to show some signs of affection towards him! But such prima-donna tantrums are only to be expected of truly great stars and, as if to prove the point, Orangey's career continued with the part of **Minerva** in the TV series *Our Miss Brooks* and, as a crowning achievement, a second classic Patsy-winning performance as Holly Golightly's cat in *Breakfast at Tiffany's* (1962). (**Patsy**, **Ray**, **Tiffany**)

Disney's real cats

As well as animation, the Walt Disney studios have also produced a number of live-action films starring cats, two of which have featured Patsy-winning performances by their leading actors. In *That Darn Cat* (1961) the Siamese cat (played by **Syn Cat**) finds its services called upon by the FBI; and **Amber** plays the role of spaceship commander **Jake** in *The Cat From Outer Space* (1978). Other cat movies by Disney include *Three Lives of Thomasina* based on the Paul Gallico novel and *The Incredible Journey*, from the story of a Siamese and two dogs by Sheila Burnford. (*Jake*, *Thomasina*, *Sheila*)

Arthur, the Kattomeat king

The first really big feline TV commercial star — both in the UK and the USA — was a pure white British Shorthair female by the name of **Samantha**, owned by the actress June Clyne. Samantha's remarkable talent was the ability to scoop catfood out of a tin using her left paw, and when the advertising agency handling Spillers Kattomeat heard of this they signed up the clever cat and renamed her **Arthur** to replace a less gifted tom who currently starred in their campaign. 'Arthur' and the catfood were an instant success and between 1966 and 1975 the cat appeared in over 30 different commercials — 'voices' being supplied by famous actors such as Leo McKern and Joss Ackland — before dying in February 1976 aged 16.

However, Arthur's fame was not confined to the screen as a tremendous *cause célèbre* ensued when June Clyne fell mortally ill and Spillers tried to buy the moneyspinning star. Not only Clyne's mother in Australia but also her partner Anthony Manning fought public battles in the press claiming ownership. Eventually, Spillers paid off both parties and all seemed to be settled until Manning issued a writ claiming loss of earnings from a company who wished to make glass models of Arthur.

He then managed to obtain a court order giving him custody of the cat which he subsequently claimed to have hidden in the Russian embassy. Not surprisingly this instantly became headline news across the world, and was particularly well publicized in the USA where Arthur now featured as a cartoon. Spillers fought back and when Manning refused to hand over the cat he was imprisoned with even more publicity, alleging that Spillers had pulled some of Arthur's teeth. Eventually the situation was resolved and Arthur returned to the screen.

Fan mail from her adoring public never ceased during Arthur's lifetime and all letters were answered, each one signed with a rubber stamp in the shape of a paw print. After her death a specially trained two-year-old, Arthur II, took over in January 1987. (*Joss*)

Walk-on cats

Leaving aside such misleading feline fripperies as Jane Fonda's character **Cat Ballou** and Goldfinger's personal pilot **Pussy Galore**, played by Honor Blackman in the James Bond film of the same name, a number of real cats have appeared in cameo roles in the movies.

It is of course a cat that betrays the presence of the supposedly dead Harry Lime in *The Third Man*, and Ellie Creed's pet, **Church**, whose death and resurrection presage a landslide of horror in Stephen King's *Pet Sematary*. And in *The Goldwyn Follies* over 300 cats overwhelm a theatrical agent in his office.

This latter film caused a rumpus at the time as a representative of the US Humane Education League in Los Angeles claimed that the cats were worked unreasonable hours, from 8a.m. to 7p.m., and were driven around the studio by means of an air hose. As a result, the British Board of Film Censors insisted that the scene be cut, but relented later when the British Consul cabled from California to give his personal assurance that there had been no cruelty.

The Bond cats

There must be something rather evil about white chinchillas for in both *You Only Live Twice* and *Diamonds Are Forever*, the archvillain Bloefeld appears stroking one — in reality that fine feline actor **Solomon**. But no matter what goes on around him the cat, like his double-0 opponent, is at most shaken, not stirred. (*Bloefeld, James*)

Tonto and the heroes

In the film *Harry and Tonto*, Harry Combes (played by a bespectacled Art Carney) is a 72-year-old retired teacher living in Manhattan with his beloved cat, a big ginger tom called **Tonto**. The two have a close rapport and when one day they are evicted from their apartment they decide to head west together in an old car. En route they have a number of adventures and Tonto develops a taste for long, filled rolls known as 'hero sandwiches'. However, when they reach California Tonto catches a virus and dies. For outstanding services to the cinema Tonto won a Patsy award for this role in 1975.

Morris, the American Dream cat

There was never a better example of a true rags-to-riches story than that of **Morris**, star of the 9-Lives catfood commercials in the USA. Spotted by a talent scout as a down-and-out stray holed up in a cat shelter near Chicago, the 15lb orange-striped tom was soon strutting his stuff in front of an audience of millions. Named Morris by the Leo Burnett advertising agency who handled the 9-Lives account, they also gave the fussy cat a voice saying 'The cat who doesn't act finicky soon loses control of its owner'. And the rest, as they say, is history. In a 10-year career Morris appeared in 40 TV advertisements, starred in the film *Shamus* and was the first animal of any kind to win a Patsy award for acting in TV commercials. Morris died in 1978 and

was succeeded by Morris II, again discovered in a cats' home. (*Shamus*)

Cat horror films

Cats have also starred in horror movies including *The Black Cat* (1941), based on Edgar Allan Poe's grisly tale; *Eye of the Cat* (1969), and the chilling *The Night of the Thousand Cats*, in which murderous moggies munch maidens in a madman's castle! Less horrific is *Bell, Book and Candle* in which **Pyewacket** (who won a Patsy for the performance in 1959) is the Siamese 'familiar' of the witch Gillian Holroyd in this lighthearted film based on the play by John van Druten.

EXOTICS AND
RARE BREEDS

Antigone — After **Tarawood** Antigone, a brown Burmese, who gave birth to the biggest litter of kittens on record — 19 — in Oxfordshire in 1970.

Archy/Archangel — Archangel is where Russian Blues originated from.

Baroness — For Baroness von Ulman who first developed the Havana Brown breed in the early 1950s.

Belle — Champion Belle of Bradford was the first registered American Shorthair cat in the USA. Born 1 June 1900 it was, despite its name, a *male* red tabby.

Bismarck/Disraeli/Gladstone — Persians owned by Florence Nightingale. (*Florence*)

Blazer — After the 1986 British Supreme Grand Champion Pannaduloa Blazer, a male red-point Siamese.

Boyo — A Welsh or Cymric cat.

Brillo — For a wire-haired breed.

Calvin — After a large Maltese with a white underside owned by Harriet Beecher Stowe (see *Cats of the Famous*). (*Harriet*)

Calypso — Prefix for a number of prize-winning Burmese cats in Britain belonging to top breeder Mrs Walker of Kent

— or for any puss that likes a good song.

Cameo — For a Cameo Longhair breed.

Captain — After Captain **Jenks**, one of the earliest recorded Maine Coon types, so called because of the early theory that they had been mated with racoons (see *Weird, Wild and Wonderful Cats*).

Chango — After a famous male Burmese that had considerable impact on British pedigrees.

Chinnie — 'Mother of the Chinchillas' Chinnie, owned by Mrs Valence, was the first ever Chinchilla Persian, and an ancestor of the famous Silver Lambkin.

Chiquita — La Chiquita was the first US champion Himalayan cat after the breed was officially recognized in 1957.

Clinker — A large Persian that appears in the novel *The Case of the Caretaker's Cat* by Erle Stanley Gardner.

Crinkles — For a Rex.

Crispin — From the Latin for 'curly-haired' — for a Rex variety.

Cupid — Cupid **Bassajio** was the first recorded Persian Cream. Born in 1890, it was a big male with tabby markings and bars.

Curly — After Kirlee, an early Devon Rex, or for any curly-haired cat.

Cyrus — The Persian word for 'sun' — so for a golden longhair.

Daffy — Familiar name of Casa Gatos da **Foong**, the first Burmese ever exhibited in Britain (November 1949) which created great interest and was shown on TV.

Droopy — For a Scottish Fold type.

Emery — For any rough-backed cat (e.g. Rex) after the nail-file boards.

Flopsy — Flopsy was one of Peter Rabbit's sisters in Beatrix Potter's series of children's books, but the name would well suit a Scottish Fold with similar floppy ears.

Foss — After the stubby-tailed cat owned by Edward Lear (see *Cats of the Famous*).

Frosty — For a lilac-point Siamese with frosty grey points; for a cat with white or pale edges to its ears, eyebrows or tail; or simply for any cat that seems to be so cold that it's always asleep in front of the fire!

Godiva — For a Mexican Hairless, after the legendary Lady Godiva (d. 1080), wife of Leofric, Earl of Mercia, who rode naked through Coventry in order to obtain remission for the townspeople from the heavy taxes imposed by her husband. A very naked lady. (*Leofric*)

Gri-Gri — The name of French President Raymond Poincaré's Siamese (see *Cats of the Famous*). (*Poincaré*)

Harrison — After Harrison Weir, 'the Father of the Cat Fancy' in Britain, who organized the world's first ever cat show in 1871.

Humbert — Mr E Barker actually refused $1000 for his cat Lord Humbert when it arrived in the USA in 1885 and caused a sensation — and that was when $50 was a high price for a cat. For a sensational cat.

Imran — An Asiatic superstar type, after the Pakistani cricketer.

José/Pépé — Manx cats are believed to derive from tailless cats from a Spanish galleon that foundered on Spanish Rock near the Isle of Man during the Armada in 1558 — hence a good Iberian name is appropriate.

Kallibunker — After the first ever Cornish Rex, bred in the UK by Mrs Ennismore in 1950 (see *Weird, Wild and Wonderful Cats*).

Kittery — After a town in Maine, USA — for a Maine Coon.

Kojak — For a hairless cat, after the TV detective played by Telly Savalas. (*Telly*)

Lamorna — For a Cornish Rex, after Lamorna Cove, the first one of the variety (female) to reach the USA.

Mandalay/Rangoon — For Burmese varieties.

Matty — For a cat with a matted coat.

Max — After King Max, a famous American Black Persian that won the Boston Cat Show in 1897, 1898 and 1899.

Miranda — Latin for 'admirable' and also after Baroness Miranda von Kirchberg who bred the first Burmillas.

Misty Malarky Ying Yang — The name of a Siamese owned by US President Carter's daughter, Amy (see *Cats of the Famous*). (*Carter, Amy*)

Mr Wu — For a Peke-Faced Persian.

Peta — The first female Home Office cat in a long line of male Peters stretching back to 1883. This black Manx was presented by the Isle of Man government in 1964.

Pickford — For a Turkish Van?

Piskie — The Cornish name for a pixie; for a Rex.

Princess — For an Egyptian Mau, the only spotted domestic breed, after Princess Troubestskoy who first introduced them into the USA in 1957 — or for any classy cat. (*Troubestskoy*)

Princess Truman Tai-Tai — After the famous Siamese of this name who travelled the world with the crew of the ship *Sagamire* (see *Record-Breaking Cats*).

Pushkin — A pleasant name for a poetic pussy, after Russia's greatest poet Alexander Pushkin, so perhaps for a Russian Blue? The eminent philosopher John

McTaggart also owned a cat by this name for which he would happily give up his only chair, to sit on the floor and think about the Absolute. (*McTaggart*)

Pyewacket — Siamese star of the film *Bell, Book and Candle* (see *Screen Cats*).

Rajah — Owned by the cat-writer Frances Simpson, this prize-winning Brown Tabby Persian was the best-known stud of his day. Also the Burmese name for Burmese cats which dwelt in Buddhist temples as early as the 15th century. (*Frances*)

Rama — After King Rama V of Thailand who supposedly named the Korat cat.

Rasamba — After a famous Abyssinian which was sent to Canada and stolen when its owner Mrs Burnford (whose Siamese was the cat in *The Incredible Journey*) was on holiday in Miami in the 1940s. Widespread TV and press coverage failed to produce its return and there are now a lot of Abyssinians in the USA!

Rifan Sabishi — The female Abyssinian for whom chef Richard Graham wrote the book, *Cuisine for Cats* (see *A Cat Miscellany*). (*Graham*)

Rochford — After the breeder Mrs Rochford, who is to be thanked for having managed to keep Russian Blues from dying out completely in the UK during World War II.

Rocky — A good name for a Maine Coon, after Rocky Racoon in the Paul McCartney song.

Roo — Manx cats are also called 'kangaroo cats' from their strange, rabbit-like gait, deriving from the fact that their hind legs are longer than their forelegs.

Ruffie — After Birkdale Ruffie, a superior Brown Tabby Persian awarded an autographed photograph of Edward VII when Prince of Wales (presented by the prince himself at Crystal Palace in 1896).

Russell — For a Birman, after Major Gordon Russell who

introduced the breed to France in 1919.

Sabra — Prefix used for a number of prize-winning cats bred by Moira Swift (*sabra* is Hebrew for 'to rest', which is very appropriate for a constantly sleeping cat). (*Moira*)

Saha — After the strong-minded Russian Blue in Colette's story 'The Cat' that has no intention of giving up her master to his new wife (see *Fictional Cats*). (*Colette*)

Salaam — A Muslim salutation meaning 'peace', but also from the title of the film *Salaam Bombay*, for a Bombay or a generally peaceful type.

Sawat — *Si-Sawat* is the local Thai name for a Korat cat.

Sean — For a short-haired breed, a Mexican Hairless or Sphynx, or any variety that looks as if it has been shorn!

Shan — The Siamese owned by Susan Ford, daughter of US President Gerald Ford (see *Cats of the Famous*). (*Susan, Gerald*)

Shuang-Mei — (See *Classical and Classy Cats.*)

Sinh — After the beautiful Birman cat owned by the head priest of the Burmese Temple of Lao-Tsun which legend says put its paws on its master when raiders killed him while praying and changed from white to the colour of Birmans, refused all food and died seven days later (see *Legendary Cats*). (*Lao-Tsun*)

Sparky — A good name for the extraordinary American Wirehair, or alternatively for any of the long-haired breeds (e.g. Persian Black) whose coats store up static electricity and can give you a shock when stroking or combing (one of the reasons why cats are associated with witches).

Susie — The name of the first ever Scottish Fold, bred by William and Mary Ross. (*Ross*)

Syn Cat — Siamese star of the film *That Darn Cat* (see *Screen Cats*).

Taffy — For a Cymric or Welsh cat? Or after Taffy the Topaz Cat who 'thinks of this and now of that,/But chiefly of his meals' in the poem by Christopher Morley. (*Morley*)

Tai-Tai — (See 'Princess Truman Tai-Tai'.)

Tao — After the male Siamese star of Sheila Burnford's book *The Incredible Journey*. (*Sheila*)

Thumbelina — For a Turkish Van, after the white thumb-mark on its head supposed to be Allah's thumbprint, and also after the fairytale.

Tiffany — Another name for a long-haired Burmese.

Tonks — For a Tonkinese.

Trelawny — A good Cornish name for a Rex.

Vashka — The name of Tsar Nicholas I's Russian Blue.

Vichien — The *vichien mas* was a type of Siamese recorded in the 14th-century *Cat Book Poems*, a manuscript held in the National Library of Thailand in Bangkok.

Voodoo — After Vel-vene Voo Doo of Silva-Wyte, a supreme champion and British Cat of the Year in 1959. One of the best Persian Blacks on record he also sired an enormous number of kittens.

Wegie/Weegie — Familiar name for the Norwegian Forest Cat or Skaukatt.

Wong-Mau — The first Burmese brought to the USA, in 1930.

Woody — For a Norwegian Forest Cat, any brown variety, or a comic puss (after Woody Allen).

Yul — For a hairless cat, after the bald actor Yul Brynner.

Zahran — Described by the Australian *Woman's Weekly* magazine in 1953 as 'the uncrowned king of Burmese in Britain', Zahran was the first Burmese to be seen in Australia.

Zaida — A peerless Chinchilla Persian owned by Lady Decies and receiver of many awards.

Zula — The first Abyssinian in the UK.

WEIRD, WILD AND WONDERFUL CATS

Cats with wings

One of the most extraordinary phenomena in the feline world is the occurrence of winged cats. The first report of these weird aberrations appeared in the 'Curiosities' feature in the November 1899 issue of the *Strand Magazine*, accompanied by a photograph of an unfortunate beast apparently purring away on a rug, completely oblivious to the furry chicken-wing-like growths that sprouted from its tabby back. The owner, a woman from Wivelscombe in Somerset, stated that it began life as a normal kitten and that the wings sprouted later. Several other cases of winged cats have been recorded worldwide including examples in Oxford (1933) and Sheffield (1939) in the UK and a number in the USA. A 20lb specimen, with a wingspan of 23 inches, was shot in Sweden in 1949 after apparently swooping down onto a child.

Tabbies

Tabby cats are now extremely common in Europe and America but this wasn't always the case. The original Old English cat was apparently blue-black and white, and tabbies didn't arrive in England until the late 1630s. Indeed, one of the first owners of a tabby was the cat-loving Archbishop of Canterbury William Laud, whose persecution of the Puritans eventually led to the English Civil War and his own execution — perhaps he'd have been better off with a black cat!

The word 'tabby' itself is supposed to derive from Attabiah, part of old Baghdad, where they used to make watered silk which had a similar pattern to the cat's coat and when first imported to the UK was known as 'atabis' or 'tabbi' silk. (*Laud, Attabiah*)

The drain cat

The smallest breed of domestic cat is the Singapura or 'Drain Cat', so-called because of its habitat in the streets of Singapore. The average weight of an adult male is only 6lb, which, bearing in mind the size of some rats, must cause the Malaysian moggy a few problems!

Cats or dogs?

A number of instances have been recorded of canine behaviour amongst cats over the years and one breed in particular — the Peke-faced Persian — even looks like one. The earliest instances of these doggy propensities are recorded by the ancient Egyptians, who used cats when out hunting. On a tomb at Thebes a cat is depicted 'pointing' at a bird in the classic manner whilst its master aims a stick at his prey. And on another tomb discovered in the same place, and now in the British Museum, a cat is shown actually retrieving waterfowl in its mouth.

W.H. Hudson, in his *The Book of a Naturalist*, also describes seeing a black cat running with the dogs to retrieve game whilst out shooting one day, and Carl van Vechten, author of *The Tiger in the House*, had a cat called **Ariel** that would fetch and return a thrown catnip mouse. Has the dog finally had his day? (*Carl*)

A beetle-browed cat

One of the more unusual features of the Egyptian Mau cat, apart from its slanting oriental eyes, is the furry pattern be-

tween its ears. These markings bear a remarkable resemblance to the scarab beetle — a sacred creature in ancient Egypt and reproduced on amulets and in hieroglyphics as a symbol of the sun god. Significant though this may be, in reality the scarab is nothing more than the common dung beetle which seems an odd thing to wear as a crown... (*Scarab*)

Odd-eyed cats

One of the most curious afflictions of cats is having eyes of different colours. In *Rogue Herries* by Hugh Walpole, the only friend of the reputed witch Katherine Wilson is a 'great grey cat with one green eye and one brown'. However, the Odd-eyed White — a large long-haired variety — is now an officially recognized breed, but the eye colouring is critical: one must be blue, the other orange. Presumably a stop-go combination of red and green would cause too much chaos at night!

Swimming cats

Who says cats don't like water? One of the best-known bathing varieties is the auburn-and-white Turkish Van, so-called after Lake Van in Turkey where, in 1955, a number were discovered happily paddling around. Manx cats are also not averse to a quick dip if the water's not too chilly, but the most famous aquatic moggy was a black-and-white Persian from St Mary's in the Scilly Isles. A regular swimmer between boats in the harbour in his youth, later in life he would sit in the sea every night and catch fish with his paws.

And whilst on the subject of angling felines, one notable example was owned by the Russian composer Borodin whose male tabby, **Rybolov** ('fisherman'), used to break holes in ice-covered lakes and hook up fish through them with his paws. Which I suppose just goes to show that it's not just Scilly cats who get their feet wet! (*Borodin*)

Flat-headed cats

Looking like something that has tangled with cartoonist Simon Bond (*101 Uses for a Dead Cat*), this very rare and strange feline is a native of southern Asia and is dark brown with a white underside. Only 20 inches long, it is one of the world's smallest cats and is distinguished by its flat skull and small, wide-spaced ears. However, any suggestion that its diminutive cranial dome has resulted from excessive domestication and repeated head-patting would be misleading, as this cat is still largely wild and is a stout fighter.

Brillo-backed cats

One of the more unusual breeds of cat is the Cornish Rex, which first appeared in Cornwall in 1950. The father of them all, **Kallibunker**, was covered in curly fur — even its whiskers were crimped! — and it had a wedge-shaped head. The Devon Rex followed some years later, and differs in having a slight kink in its nose and wavier fur. But the cat with the coarsest coat of all is the American Wire Hair, which is tough enough to put you off stroking the cat altogether!

Naked cats

A number of rare breeds have now become extinct and doubt begins to creep in as to whether the Chinese Drop-eared cat or a true albino ever really existed. However, one species whose final days were well documented was the Mexican Hairless. The last pair of these was owned by F.J. Shinick of Albuquerque, New Mexico, and described by him in a letter in 1902. A present from a local Indian tribe they were apparently the last of a long line of Aztec cats and were very intelligent and affectionate. Their unique feature, as the name indicates, was the total lack of body hair. Instead, both were covered in a loose, mousy skin which was soft to the touch, and the neck, stomach and legs

were flesh-coloured. **Nellie**, the female, had amber eyes, a voice like a child's and weighed 8lb. **Dick** was rather heavier and in the winter both grew a light fur on their backs and on the ridge of their tails. Sadly, Dick escaped from the house one day and was killed by a dog, and when Nellie died the breed became extinct — Mr Shinick hadn't allowed them to mate as they were brother and sister.

However, a new variety of nude cat has recently appeared on the scene. The offspring originally of an ordinary domestic black-and-white cat in Ontario, the Canadian Hairless or Sphynx Cat has large ears, golden eyes and no hair on its body except for the tip of its tail. It also differs from the Mexican breed by having no whiskers.

The boneless cat

A rather extraordinary type of cat is the popular US Ragdoll breed. A mixture of Angora, Birman and Burmese it has the general appearance of a long-haired Siamese and can weigh up to 20lb. An extremely docile cat, it has the unusual ability to hang completely limp if carried, rather like a child's rag doll, and is no doubt the variety Snoopy encounters dangling from a neighbour's arm in Charles Schulz's *You Can't Win, Charlie Brown* (Vol.1). Justifiably alarmed by the appearance of the creature his only comment is 'Amazing...they've finally developed a boneless cat!'

Webb-footed felines

Mention has already been made of domestic cats that have learnt to fish for their supper, but in the swamps of India, Malaysia and Sri Lanka there lurks a true Fishing Cat which has slightly webbed feet adapted to its task. Weighing about 22lb this Isaak Walton of the cat world is generally a tawny-grey colour and is about 2½ feet long with a stout body and short legs.

The cat's pyjamas

The sacred Japanese Bobtail cat was first introduced into the USA in the 1960s and is also known as the Kimono cat because of the patterning of its tricoloured black, red and white coat which resembles this popular garment. Like the Manx its hindlegs are longer than its forelegs and it has a unique tail which appears to be a stump but in fact is tightly curled and when stretched out is about 4 inches long.

Racoon cats

The very handsome and popular Maine Coon cat from the USA is, with the Ragdoll, the largest domestic breed and owes its name to the belief that it developed as a cross between a cat and a racoon. This myth finds some substance in the coloration of its coat, which certainly resembles the banded creature. However, apparently an attempt to end the dispute by inducing a domestic moggy to mate with a wild racoon only resulted in an almighty dust-up and much loss of fur! So the fantasy remains. A more likely explanation is that it is a cross between indigenous US cats and Asiatic long-haired varieties introduced to the country by sailors via the New England port of Maine.

CLASSICAL AND CLASSY CATS

Abigail — Meaning a handmaiden, for a devoted female.

Abra — One of Solomon's favourites in the Bible, the heroine of the 16th-century romance, *Amadis of Gaul*, and the Hebrew word for 'mother of multitudes' (the male equivalent is **Abraham**). For a very productive lady cat of some refinement.

Ailuros — Greek for 'cat'.

Aladdin — A lamp-loving type?

Alexander — Alexander the Great was known as 'the winged leopard' — thus a good name for an all-conquering cat that moves like lightning.

Alfonso — After the Italian poet Alfonso Gatto (cat).

Apollo — Greek god of light, poetry, music, healing and prophecy and a name for a strikingly handsome youth...

Apollyon — The destroyer (from the Greek).

Arden/MacKay — The oldest pedigree families in England and Scotland, respectively.

Ariel/Ariella — Ancient Hebrew name meaning 'lion/lioness of God', and perhaps, with a touch of Shakespeare's character from *The Tempest*, a rather ethereal one.

Ashtoreth — A terrible destructive Syrian goddess of war with the head of a lioness who drives a four-horse chariot.

Aslan — Aslan is the Great Lion in C.S. Lewis's 'Chronicles of Narnia' series. He created Narnia, gave its animals the power of speech and brought English children there to fight the powers of evil.

Atossa — After Matthew Arnold's cat. (*Matthew*)

Avatar — The manifestation of a deity in human or animal form in Hindu mythology.

Ayesha/Aisha — The favourite wife of Mohammed and the central figure in Rider Haggard's novel. (*Mohammed*)

Balthus — After the painter of the self-portrait, *The King of Cats*.

Barocci — A leading Italian artist in the second half of the 16th century who deserves to be immortalized if only for his painting of the *Madonna del Gatto*, showing the Virgin with a cat.

Bast — After the Egyptian cat goddess (see *Legendary Cats*).

Beatrix/Beatrice — A perfect name for a cat as it means 'she who makes others happy' in Latin. It is also the name of Dante's heroine in the 13th-century *Divine Comedy* (Beatrice) and Beatrix Potter's marvellous children's stories feature many immortal cat characters.

Blake — William Blake wrote the poem 'The Tyger'; Blake Edwards directed *The Pink Panther*.

Bodo — After the poet Charles Baudelaire, a well-known cat-lover. (*Baudelaire*)

Bouhaki — A cat owned by the Egyptian King Hana (c. 11th century). One of the earliest representations of a cat, Bouhaki is depicted at the feet of the king's statue in the Necropolis at Thebes. (*Hana*)

Boz — A Dickensian cat — *Scratches by Boz*?

Calgacus — The earliest recorded name in Scotland (c. AD 40), perhaps for a Scottish Fold?

Calton — Christopher Tietjens's cat in Ford Madox Ford's *Parade's End*.

Calverley — After C. S. Calverley who wrote the cat poem 'Sad Memories'.

Carl — 'Carl-cat' is the old-fashioned way of describing a tom-cat, i.e. a boar- or he-cat. From the Anglo-Saxon *carle* meaning 'male'.

Casanova/Don Juan — Sexy males.

Caterina — Edgar Allan Poe's cat (see *Cats of the Famous*).

Catullus — For a poetic puss.

Chanoine — Victor Hugo's cat (see *Cats of the Famous*). (**Hugo**)

Childebrand — One of Théophile Gautier's cats (see *Cats of the Famous*).

Clotilde — After Clotilde of the Burgundians, wife of the great Clovis, King of the Franks, whose emblem was a sable cat killing a rat (5th century). (**Clovis**)

Crichton — An admirable type, after the butler in J. M. Barrie's play.

Cunningham — After World War II air ace, 'Cat's Eyes' Cunningham.

Cybele — Cybele was a Phrygian goddess whose chariot was drawn by two lions.

Divitiacus — A Gaulish ruler of Kent in c. 75 BC and the earliest recorded British name (also known as **Prydhain**).

Echo — For a cat that you keep calling and all you ever hear is your own voice!

Elsa — Lioness star of Joy Adamson's books *Born Free, Living Free* and *Forever Free* as well as a feature film and a TV series, Elsa was rescued as a cub and brought up in the Adamsons' house. She was later returned to the wild where she mated and had cubs but would still visit the Adamsons' camp until she died in 1961. (*Elsa* is Old German for 'noble one' — the name of the legendary bride of

Lohengrin.) (*Joy, Lohengrin*)

Epicurus — A fastidious eater.

Eponine — Another cat owned by Gautier (see *Cats of the Famous*).

Eric — After Eric Gurney, one of the most perceptive of animal cartoonists, who refuses to humanize his subjects. He is best known for his successful book *How to Live With a Calculating Cat* (1962).

Firapeel — After the leopard which appears in the 12th-century story, *Roman de Renart*.

Freya — The Scandinavian goddess Freya's chariot was drawn by two cats (see *Legendary Cats*).

Furioz — A general descriptive name for cats used by St Albertus Magnus, the 13th-century scholar and teacher of Thomas Aquinas. (*Aquinas*)

Galahad — A romantic type, after the Arthurian Knight of the Round Table.

Gattullo/Jatta — Two Italian dialect forms of the word for 'cat'.

Gavroche — One owned by Théophile Gautier (see *Cats of the Famous* and *Personalities*).

Gazette — After one of Cardinal Richelieu's cats (see *Cats of the Famous*).

Gunduple — The name of the goblin-eating cat in an old legend from Borneo (see *Legendary Cats*).

Gyp/Gypsy — Originally meaning 'Egyptian', this would be an appropriate name for a creature that was so adored by this ancient race. Gyp was also 'a nefarious old cat' owned by Andrew Lang, author of *The Blue Fairy Book* etc., and Gip belonged to the poet W. H. Hudson. (**Hudson**)

Hamilcar/Hannibal — Hamilcar Barca was a great Carthaginian general who fought against the Romans in the 3rd century BC, and was the father of the legendary Hannibal who crossed the Alps by elephant. Hamilcar was also the name of a cat owned by Anatole France and features in his first successful book, *Le Crime de Sylvestre Bonnard* (see *Fictional Cats*). For unconventional types who like a good scrap. (**Anatole**)

Harry — After two cats, Oil-Can Harry who is the top-hatted villain in Terrytoons' Mighty Mouse animated cartoon series, and Harry Cat, a striped tom who lives in a drainpipe in the Times Square subway station in New York in the books by George Selden.

Hasan — Excavations at Beni Hasan, a town 100 miles from Cairo, led to the discovery of an enormous cat graveyard. Literally thousands of mummified cats were found (see *A Cat Miscellany*).

Heracles/Hercules — One of the tasks of Hercules (the first, in fact) was to slay the Nemean Lion which was reputed to have an invulnerable skin. Hercules strangled the beast, skinned it and is usually seen wearing the pelt in most

depictions. Incidentally, another of the great hero's labours was to frighten away the Stympalian Birds, which made a terrific racket — a task well suited to a brave cat!

Hidden-Kissa — This is the cat owned by the odious giant Hiisi in Finnish mythology. Though she caused terror wherever she went, she did some good in that she forced thieves to confess their misdeeds. (*Hiisi*)

Hotspur — A fiery, impetuous puss, after Sir Henry 'Hotspur' Percy.

Howel — After cat-loving monarch Howel the Good (see *Legendary Cats*).

Huxley — Aldous Huxley wrote *Sermons on Cats*. (*Aldous*)

Irena — After Irena Dubrovna, the Serbian cat-woman in the horror film *Cat People*.

Jennie/Thomasina — After the feline stars of the books by Paul Gallico.

Jeoffrey — After Christopher Smart's puss in the famous poem.

Kazza — Old High German for 'cat'.

Khan — According to Marco Polo, the great Kublai Khan used to hunt with trained leopards, lynxes and lions, so this would be a name with excellent feline credentials. (*Marco, Kublai*)

Kliban — Named after the cat cartoonist, B. Kliban.

Koshka — Russian for 'cat'.

Lara — Latin for 'shining famous one' and Etruscan for 'lordly'. Also, as in Roman mythology Lara was the daughter of the river god Almo, perhaps a suitable name for a cat that plays with water in the sink? (*Almo*)

Louisa — A cat owned by the writer William Makepeace Thackeray (see *Cats of the Famous*). (*Thackeray*)

Lyncus — According to Ovid's *Metamorphoses* (Book V), Lyncus, King of Scythia, was turned into a lynx by Ceres for trying to kill Triptolemus. (*Ceres, Triptolemus*)

Margaras — Sanskrit name for a cat, deriving from *margas* or 'track' and hence he who follows the track, a hunter, investigator. An identical Hindi word, but with different accents, derives from the root 'to cleanse' (i.e. cats cleanse homes of mice and rats).

Marsay/de Marsay — After the cat immortalized in J. K. Stephens's poem 'Elegy on de Marsay'.

Martelli — After a kind of wildcat, now extinct, called Martelli's Cat.

Martin — After cat painter, Martin Leman.

Maverick — A bit of a tearaway.

Melchior — As well as being one of the Magi or Three Wise Men of the Bible (along with **Caspar** and **Balthazar**) — in itself good enough precedent for a cat name — Melchior was also the Christian name of the famous 16th-century master printer of Venice, Sessa, whose printer's mark depicted a cat with a rat in its mouth set under a crown. (*Sessa*)

Meuzza — The cat of the prophet Mohammed.

Min — After Thoreau's feline companion (see *Cats of the Famous*). (*Thoreau*)

Ming — The Ming Dynasty in China lasted from 1368 to 1644 and its porcelain is characterized by the use of brilliant colours and fine-quality body. No doubt Patricia Highsmith's cat in *Ming's Biggest Prey* also possessed some of these qualities.

Minna — After publisher Michael Joseph's Minna Minna Mowbray (he also had a cat called **Charles**).

Molly Mog — The pretty publican's daughter in Gay's poem.

Mowcher — The dwarf hairdresser in *David Copperfield* — for a small preening type.

Musion — A common old name for a cat (literally 'mouse-killer').

Nakulus — The Sanskrit word for an ichneumon meaning,

literally, 'destroyer of nocturnal mice' — sounds like a good name for a cat?

Nellie — One celebrated in verse by Hartley Coleridge.

Nemo — Latin for 'nobody' and after Harold Wilson's Siamese.

Nico — The shepherd's cat 'with lions curbed clawe' in *Second Eclogues of Arcadia* by Sir Philip Sidney (1554-86).

Nubbles — After Kit Nubbles from Dickens's *The Old Curiosity Shop*.

Pangloss — For a cat that's all tongue (*pan gloss* in Greek), after the philosopher in Voltaire's *Candide*. (**Voltaire**)

Patripatan — After the celestial cat of India (see *Legendary Cats*).

Pharaoh — As the Egyptians were so keen on cats, any cat would be honoured to take the title of their kings. Perhaps something along the lines of **Watapet I** might be suitable!

Pietro — After Pietro della Valle, the 16th-century Italian traveller who reputedly introduced long-haired cats to Europe from Asia Minor.

Pinky/Paul — Not after the pig puppets **Pinky** and **Perky** (though these would be good names for twin cats) but for an ultra-cool Pink Panther-type cat. Originally created by Fritz Freleng for animated credits to Blake Edwards's comedy involving a jewel thief, the *Pink Panther* cartoon quickly took on a life of its own and United Artists released a number of animated shorts, followed by a TV series. The panther, who walks upright, never speaks in the films and is not named (though German comic books talk of 'Paulchen der Rosarote Panther'). *The Pink Phink* won an Academy Award in 1964.

Pip — For a cat with 'great expectations', after the Dickens character.

Ra — After the Egyptian sun god who is often depicted as a cat (see *Legendary Cats*).

Ribby — A cat that appears in a number of Beatrix Potter stories.

Saladin — An all-conquering Asian variety, after the great warrior who faced the Crusaders in the 12th century.

Scaramouche — The boastful coward in *commedia dell'arte*.

Sekhmet — The Egyptian lion-goddess, sometimes also portrayed with a cat's head. Whereas Bast shows the kindly warming power of the sun, Sekhmet personifies its terrifying, scorching heat. Sekhmet is also, by coincidence, the oldest recorded name of an Egyptian king, dating from before 3050 BC.

Shuang-Mei — A cat owned by Chu Hou-Tsung, 11th Emperor of the Chinese Ming Dynasty in the 16th century. The cat was so-called because it was faintly blue with white eyebrows (the name means 'frost eyebrows'). For an oriental breed that appears used to walking around palaces. (*Chu, Hou-Tsung*)

Sidrophel — Meaning 'star-lover'.

Sinclair — After Sinclair Lewis (1855-1951) who wrote, amongst other great works, 'The Cat's Prayer' that begins 'Ancient of days/With whiskers torrendous,/Hark to our praise,/Lick and defend us...'

Sinny — After Maurice Sinet, known as Siné, a great cat cartoonist whose work has appeared worldwide in punning collections such as *Scatty*. Born in Paris in 1928, Siné was greatly influenced by Steinberg and has produced animated films, posters and stage sets. (*Maurice*)

Sizi — Albert Schweitzer's cat. (*Schweitzer*)

Stevens — After pop star Cat Stevens.

Sylvia — The heroine of Sandy Wilson's comic illustrated novel, *This is Sylvia*, in which the cat becomes an actress after her mother runs off to California with cat-magnate **Cyrus T. Rocksalmonfeller**. Sylvia eventually makes the big time, upstages Hollywood star **Miaow-Miaow Latouche**

and marries **Sir Algernon Gutts-Whyting**. (See *Fictional Cats*.)

Templar — After the 12th-century Knights Templar military order which was closed down by Philip the Fair of France after accusations of heresy and allegations that Satan himself appeared before them in the guise of a black cat at midnight meetings. Also perhaps after Leslie Charteris's sleuth Simon 'The Saint' Templar, for a cat with curiosity. (**Philip**, **Leslie**)

Tex — After Tex Avery, whose superb animated films, especially those featuring cats — often unnamed — have given pleasure to so many (he also created Bugs Bunny, Droopy, Daffy Duck, Porky Pig, etc.). (**Bugs**)

Theodor — After Theodor Geisel (Dr Seuss) creator of the hugely successful 'Cat in the Hat' books.

Tiberius — Lytton Strachey's cat. (**Lytton**)

Tittums — A kitten owned by Jerome K. Jerome. (**Jerome**)

Tybert — The cat who outwits the fox in the 12th-century story, *Roman de Renart*.

Venus — The Roman goddess of love and also the name of a cat owned by the poet W. H. Davies (*Autobiography of a Supertramp* etc.) who wrote a number of verses on cats.

Whiskerandos — A character in Sheridan's *The Critic*.

Wilberforce — The No. 10 Downing St puss, resident during the reigns of Heath, Wilson, Callaghan and Thatcher.

Wildwood — After Kipling's 'The Cat that Walked by Himself' in the Wet Wild Woods (see *Fictional Cats*).

Willum — After Pussy Cat Willum, the TV puppet companion of Wally Whyton. (**Wally**)

Wilycat — The little boy cat-creature in the TV cartoon series *Thundercats*, based on characters by Ted Wolf. From their base, the Cats' Lair on planet Thundera, the Thundercats — futuristic superheroes with humanoid bodies, including two females **Tygra** and **Cheetara** — fight evil forces and

are summoned together by the lion-man's Sword of Omens. (**Wiley Catt** was also the shotgun-toting bobcat in the 'Pogo' comic strip produced by Walt Kelly.)

Winston — After Winston Smith in George Orwell's novel *Nineteen Eighty-Four*, whose one secret fear was rats…

Zezolla — The legendary story of 'Cinderella' goes back many centuries and was originally called 'Cinders-Cat', which is what the Ugly Sisters' sister effectively became. However, this was always just a nickname because she worked in the kitchen; her real name, revealed in some versions, is Zezolla. (**Cinders**)

RECORD-BREAKING CATS

The tale of a tail

Some cats, especially Siamese, are occasionally born with kinked or even forked tails; the Japanese Kimono cat has a curly bobtail, while Manx and Cymric cats have no tail at all. But for a truly lavish appendage, hats must come off for **Pinky** of Southgate, London, who holds the current record for growing the world's longest cat tail, measured at 14 inches in 1978. He obvious had no trouble chasing it as a kitten!

The world's richest cat

The wealthiest cat in the world was one **Charlie Chan**, an otherwise unremarkable white feline who inherited an estate worth $250,000 when his mistress, Gene Patterson of Joplin, Missouri, USA died in January 1978. The estate included a three-bedroomed house full of antiques and a 7-acre pet cemetery. Chan himself was also appointed a personal minder to care for his whims.

Britain's most affluent cat — in true rags-to-riches manner — was a former stray called **Blackie** who inherited £20,000 in 1975. A lucky black cat indeed! However, it soon became evident that with the upkeep of a detached residence complete with full-time housekeeper catering to his now fastidious gourmet lifestyle, Blackie was clearly living beyond his means and so it was decided to sell the house, put the funds in a trust and transfer his lordship to a more modest establishment for the rest of his days. (*Gene, Joplin*)

Patricia, the high-jump cat

Who says cats don't have nine lives? If the experience of a one-year-old pregnant moggy known as **Patricia** is anything to go by then the case is surely proven.

For this unfortunate cat has the dubious honour of holding the official world record for survival from a fall from a great height. In her case it was 205 feet (62m) into the freezing-cold water (49°F) of the Willamett River, USA, on 8 March 1981.

The reason? A motorist driving over St John's Bridge in Portland, Oregon, had simply tossed her over the parapet and driven on. Luckily for Patricia, two anglers fishing directly below (ironically, for cat-fish!) saw the incident and managed to rescue the badly concussed cat. They immediately carried her to a cats' protection group who rushed her straight off to a vet. The three kittens were stillborn and the mother suffered multiple contusions but remarkably little severe damage, and after emergency surgery was eventually discharged. She was subsequently adopted by a caring family who later exhibited her with considerable pride at a number of cat shows.

Cat-racing

In 1936 the first official cat racetrack was opened in Portisham, Dorset. Fifty-odd local moggies streaked round a 220-yard circuit in the first few meetings — a blur of fur chasing an electric mouse. The times were not reported, but the highest authenticated speed for a running cat has been clocked at 27 mph (over 60 yards), though this wasn't for scampering after some mechanical rodent. Another instance of cat-racing was recorded in Kent in 1949, but for some reason all tailless specimens were banned on this occasion — proving that by then the sport had already started going to the dogs.

Million-mile moggies

Next time you see a cat curled up asleep, spare some thought for all the activity it has probably gone through the previous night: courting, fighting, prowling, patrolling and generally pounding the beat. But for really active cats it would be difficult to top the Siamese **Princess Truman Tai-Tai** who in 16 years as a crew member of the British iron-ore ship *Sagamire* travelled 1½ million nautical miles. Another million-miler was **Doodles** of the White Star liner *Cedric*, and a black-and-white male called **Tom** flew 600,000 miles in two months, from Australia to Canada and from Kuwait to Jamaica, trapped in the hold of a British Airways Jumbo jet. He was eventually rescued at Heathrow Airport and returned to his anxious owner in Norfolk.

So think carefully before disturbing that snoozing feline — after all, you don't know where he's been! (*Cedric*)

Alpine cats

One of the most extraordinary cats was that adopted by the Blumlisalp mountaineering club at Kandersteg in the Swiss Alps. One day in August 1928, to the stunned surprise of all, an inquisitive feline face appeared around the door of the Club's hut situated at 9,000 feet above sea-level. Immediately befriended by the hut's keeper, the fearless feline quickly settled in at the isolated retreat. And whenever a band of climbers passed through as they picked their way up the craggy slopes of the Blumlisalphorn mountain outside, the plucky female would tag along and follow them up the freezing rock-face to the very peak, which stands at over 12,000 feet.

Another instance of a mountaineering cat was the four-month-old kitten that accompanied climbers to the top of the treacherous Matterhorn (15,000 feet) in September 1950. And in 1962 *Life* magazine reported that the keepers of the Albert Premier shelter on Mont Blanc (8,875 feet) had a kitten named

Zizou that similarly liked to hitch rides to the summit (15,782 feet). But a word of warning to owners who like to encourage their own cats' ability in this field — it may not be wise to mention these remarkable accomplishments to the firemen next time they come to coax your precious pet off a telegraph pole, tree or roof…

Dusty, the great mother

Your average mother cat probably has between two and three litters a year, maximum — depending on when you last looked in the garden shed. So imagine how the owners of **Dusty** from Texas must have felt when she produced no less than 420 furry babies between 1935 and 1952! What with food, milk and the dirt trays — not to mention the never-ending clatter of the catflap — it gives a whole new meaning to the phrase 'having kittens'.

Adolf, the Air Force cat

One of the more unusual crew members of the US Fifth Air Force in World War II was a hitchhiking Ozzie puss who first clambered aboard Ed Stelzig's cargo plane in Darwin, Australia, on 17 February 1945. As his face bore some resemblance to the infamous Great Dictator the black-and-white cat was christened **Adolf**, and during the Pacific campaign clocked up 92,140 miles and an enormous number of flying hours. A model passenger, Adolf always appeared the minute the plane's engines coughed into life and only once mistook his aircraft (he was returned from foreign parts a week later). Ever the patriot, Adolf's regular nesting spot was amongst the warmth of the radio apparatus and, despite his name, he was never caught signalling to the enemy.

Cat Methuselahs

The oldest cats on record both came from Devon: **Puss** of

Clayhidon (36) and **Ma** (34 years 5 months). A number of other notable Methuselahs in the cat longevity stakes have been claimed over the years, but authentication has not always proved satisfactory. However, a Los Angeles cat was recorded as being 33 years 4 months on its deathbed in 1955 and **Bobby** from Co. Wexford, Ireland, reached the grand old age of 32 years 3 weeks before going for his final catnap. And that's with eight lives still to run!

Monster moggies

The average domestic cat weighs between 5 and 7lb (up to 20lb for the larger breeds). But if you ever felt the strain lifting little Tibbles out of your favourite armchair think yourself lucky not to have been the owner of **Himmy** from Queensland. For this rotund Australian tabby holds the world heavyweight record at a scale-breaking 46lb $15\frac{1}{2}$ oz — imagine having that bundle of fun jump on your bed in the morning! The British record goes to Welsh-born **Poppa** at $44\frac{1}{2}$lb, whilst a ginger-and-white tom from Connecticut weighed in at 43lb to top the US heavy-cat league.

Flying cats

A tabby cat called **Jazz** was the only animal passenger aboard the airship R-34 – the first dirigible to cross the Atlantic from England to the USA but, contrary to popular belief, Charles Lindbergh did not take a cat with him on his record-breaking solo flight in the opposite direction in 1927. However, before take-off he did have his photograph taken in the cockpit of his plane, *Spirit of St Louis*, with an attractive-looking feline known as **Patsy**. The event was commemorated in a Spanish postage stamp which had Patsy in the bottom right corner watching the plane depart.

A true story reported in the American magazine *Cat Courier* in the 1920s described the case of a Californian cat that leapt on

a duck's back and was borne aloft until the frightened bird touched down again. And conversely the *Manchester Evening News* ran a story in 1939 about a cat that was stalking sparrows on Mount Ouloudagh (or as it used to be more aptly named, Mount Olym*pus*) in Turkey when an eagle, obviously judging that it should pick on something its own size, swooped down, grabbed the cat and then dropped it from a height of 400 feet. The redoubtable moggy hit the ground running — or rather tried to. Apart from a broken leg and the loss of part of its tail the cat suffered surprisingly little damage and later recovered completely from its ordeal. Though I expect it kept away from sparrows for a while . . . (**Lindbergh**)

Cold-storage cats

According to some sources, a cold-storage company in Pittsburgh, USA, once had a problem with rats which had somehow become accustomed to the extremely low temperatures of their warehouse and were destroying the stores. As an experiment they began to introduce cats into the ice-room and found that within quite a short time the feline guards were able to adapt themselves to the environment and keep down the thieves. Indeed, such was their success that the next generation of freezer cats began to develop short bushy tails, heavy fur and very long eyebrows and whiskers. However, this new breed of polar pussies were unable to cope with outside temperatures and soon fell ill if exposed to a normal climate for long periods.

PHYSICAL CHARACTERISTICS

Achilles — For a cat with a patch of white or contrasting colour on one of its back feet, like the Greek warrior Achilles's heel.

Alanna/Alina — Two variants of a name meaning 'beautiful'. Also perhaps for a water-loving cat, after the Catalina flying-boat. (*Catalina*)

Alectic — For a three-legged cat, from 'catalectic' which is a line of verse with an incomplete final foot!

Algernon — From the French meaning 'one who has whiskers'.

Bandy — A bow-legged cobby (q.v.) or for a cat with colour-banded fur.

Barbary — For a bearded type.

Bechstein — A *piano* (soft-voiced) cat or one that likes sitting on the instrument.

Beezer — A cat with a beezer smile, or, in another sense of the word, one with a remarkable nose.

Behemoth — A giant creature from Hebrew legend with a huge appetite…

Bella — Italian for 'beautiful'.

Biffo — For one that likes butting its head against yours? Also for a bear-like cat after the comic character, Biffo the Bear.

Blaze — For any cat with a white blaze mark on its forehead. (**Blaise** was also Merlin's master.)

Blimp — For a ruddy-faced bewhiskered fat white cat, after cartoonist David Low's comic creation Colonel Blimp.

Blinkers — A blinking type or one with patches over its eyes.

Blotches — A cat with areas of white or colour in its fur.

Bobby — For a cat with white feet or 'bobby-sox'.

Bones — For a skinny puss, or one that likes bones.

Boots — One with paws of a different colour to the rest of its coat (e.g. black or white). Kipling wrote a book about Boots the dog, illustrated and owned by the cartoonist, G. L. Stampa.

Bristow — For a black-suited moustachioed puss, after Frank Dickens's strip-cartoon character. The Dickens of a cat!

Bubbles — A curly-haired cat.

Budgie — A small multicoloured type with a liking for caged birds?

Bugsy — A pint-sized gangster, after Bugsy Malone.

Bunter — After Billy Bunter, for a gluttonous feline.

Buttons — For a cat with white spots in its fur, or indeed of any contrasting colour (this is what they are called technically).

Caesius — Meaning 'blue-eyed'.

Caligula — For a slightly mad but magisterial cat with little boots (the emperor's nickname came from the military boots he wore as a child).

Caruso — A melodious neuter cat, after the famous castrato opera star.

Cassiopaea — Seen from behind, the 'M' pattern on tabbies' heads is a 'W' — the same shape as this star cluster.

Cefa — C for cat!

Chenille — After the velvety cord, for a smooth cat.

Chevron — For Ragdoll or Snowshoe varieties, which both have inverted 'V' patterns on their noses.

Chunky — A big cuddly cat.

Clarence — Clarence was the star of the film *Clarence the Cross-Eyed Lion*, which led to the TV series *Daktari* (1966-9). To emphasize his viewpoint, viewers were often shown scenes in double vision. For a cross-eyed type.

Claudius — For a lame cat.

Cobby — A cobby is any short, sturdy variety on low legs, technically speaking, but it was also the name of the last cat owned by Thomas Hardy — a grey Persian with deep orange eyes — which remained by his bedside to the end. (**Hardy**)

Crookshanks — A cat with bowed legs.

Cyllopotes — Greek meaning 'zigzagged' (one of Actaeon's hounds). (**Actaeon**)

Darren — From the Gaelic for 'little one'.

Deuteronomy — For a very old cat, after T.S. Eliot's character.

Diddy — A tiny cat.

Dodders — One with pink tips, after the plant, or perhaps for a doddery old cat.

Dumbo — For a cat with big ears, after the Disney elephant.

Dumpling/Dumpy — A fat cat (especially white).

Emmet/Emett — 'Emmet' is an archaic word for an ant, so for a small type or, perhaps, after the comic artist Rowland Emett, for a whimsical puss. (**Rowland**)

Esmeralda — For a green-eyed cat (the name means 'emerald-like') and also after the cat that featured in the US strip-cartoon *Cicero's Cat* that first appeared in 1933 (Cicero was the son of Mutt in the famous *Mutt and Jeff* series). (**Cicero, Mutt, Jeff**)

Excalibur — After King Arthur's magic sword — for a razor-sharp type that refuses to be thrown out?

Falstaff — A tubby cat.

Fang — A large-toothed puss.

Figaro — A fat, comic, singing cat that's always grooming itself?

Fluff — A soft and puffy puss.

Geoffroy — A particular species of spotted wildcat is known as the Geoffroy's Cat, after its discoverer.

Gloriana — After the Virgin Queen, Elizabeth I — for a neutered female? (*Elizabeth*)

Goblin/Hobgoblin — For a wicked little sprite.

Goggles — For a cat with rings round its eyes.

Goliath — A huge cat, after the giant of the Philistines.

Goofy — For one with goofy teeth, after the slow-witted Disney character.

Gorman — From the Celtic, meaning 'blue-eyed'.

Grable — After Betty Grable, for a cat with wonderful legs! (*Betty*)

Grippeminault — This was the monstrous cat (also known as **Clawpuss**) in Rabelais's *Gargantua and Pantagruel* stories, who was Archduke of the Furrycats, a race of terrible creatures that ate little children and fed on marble stones, and who put a difficult riddle to Panurge (which he solved). For a powerful but clever puss (see also *Fictional Cats*). (*Gargantua*, *Pantagruel*, *Panurge*)

Grizzler — A grizzled old cat or one that moans a lot.

Growltiger — A one-eyed, torn-eared ruffian described by T.S. Eliot. (Also **Grumbuskin**, **Tumblebrutus**, **Gilbert** and **Lady Griddlebone**)

Gummidge — A particularly scruffy puss, after the fictional scarecrow, Worzel Gummidge.

Harold — For a one-eyed type, after the English king defeated by William the Conqueror.

Hedgehog/Holly — A couple of prickly sorts of pusscat.

Hula — A hooped cat.

Jaggers — Another long-toothed variety, or for an exhibitionist singer, after the Rolling Stones star.

Jaws — A big-mouthed moggy with a lot of teeth!

Jeep — A general-purpose (GP) cat.

Jeffreys — After the infamous hanging magistrate, Judge Jeffreys, who wore a black cap when he passed sentence. For a severe, black-capped type.

Jill — For a one-eyed cat, after the third cat in Walter de la Mare's poem 'Five Eyes'.

Jumbo — A mega-moggy.

Katnip — For one addicted to this herb (see also *Comic Cats*).

Kitbag — 'Pack up your troubles in your old kitbag and smile, smile smile...'

Kong — A giant black tom with a liking for young women?

Laces — The name for thin vertical marks that continue above the 'boot' level on cat's legs — especially noticeable in the Snowshoe breed.

Ladders — One with horizontal markings.

Lavender/Lilac — For cats with these tinges to their fur.

Lefty — All cats are southpaws...

Leviathan/Colossus/Titan/Gargantua — Classic names for a large cat.

Lilliput/Lillipuss — A miniature cat, perhaps for a Singapura breed, after Swift's creation in *Gulliver's Travels*.

Lippy — Lippy the Lion was another product of the Hanna-Barbera animation studios. A constantly bragging con-artist, his sidekick was the lugubrious hyena, Hardy Har-Har. For a loud-mouthed cat.

Lofty — For a tall or very small type.

Lucy — A 'locket' is the technical name for a patch of different colour (e.g. white) on the neck of a cat. Hence Lucy, after Lucy Locket in the nursery rhyme. Perhaps also for a ginger cat, after the red-haired comedienne, Lucille Ball.

Mademoiselle — Long-haired cats were originally called 'French cats' when first introduced to the UK, so this might be a suitable name. Also after a cat owned by J.-K. Huysmans (1848-1907) and described by him.

Maggot — A small white.

Marx — For a cat with marks?

Micropus — A tiny kitten.

Midge — A small variety with a nasty bite.

Minikin — A wee dainty thing.

Minnow — A slender diminutive type that likes water.

Moccasins — For a pale-booted cat with a very soft tread.

Muggins — A rather simple moggy.

Mugwump — A mugwump is a neutral person in politics, so perhaps for a neutered cat?

Mumps — For one with big cheeks.

Napoleon — For a small, all-conquering cat, preferably of the long-haired or 'French' variety (Napoleon, incidentally, hated cats — see *A Cat Miscellany*).

Nelson — For a courageous type, after the famous British admiral — possibly also for one lacking an eye or a leg (or both). Robert Southey, the poet, had a cat called Lord Nelson, and Nelson was also the name of one of Churchill's many cats.

Noddy — A cat that's always nodding off...

Ounce — The name for a Central Asian snow-leopard or possibly a lightweight kitten!

Paddy — For one that steps lightly on paddy feet, or one that has green eyes reminiscent of the Emerald Isle.

Pallas/Manul — The manul or Pallas cat is a type of Asian wildcat — for a really wild Burmese or Siamese?

Papaya — For a paw-paw pussy!

Patch/Patches — A blotchy sort of cat, particularly with a dark eyepatch.

Peggy — A three-legged type?

Piccolo — For a small tom (it's Italian for 'little boy'), perhaps also one with a piping voice.

Plug — For a cat with big teeth like the character in *Beano*'s 'The Bash Street Kids'; for one with histrionic tendencies, after Plug the cat who lived at the Adelphi Theatre, London; or for a red, brown and blue type after the electric wiring code!

Polypheme/Polyphemus — The one-eyed Cyclops in Homer's *Odyssey*. (**Cyclops**)

Popeye — For an exopthalmic blue-and-white cat, after the cartoon character.

Puff — A puffy puss and after a character in Balzac's *The Love Affairs of an English Cat*. (**Balzac**)

Pug — A Peke-faced type, or for a particularly pugnacious one.

Purdy/Purdey — For a pretty pussy, or one that goes off like a gun?

Quark/Atom — The tiniest of all cats.

Quasimodo — A deaf cat that likes playing with bells?

Ragtime — An offbeat, scruffy but fun cat.

Ringo — A ringed type.

Rip — A real tearaway puss, especially one that has suffered in a few fights (torn ears etc.).

Riser — Another name for a stump-tailed cat.

Rosebud — For a cat with a beautiful pink nose?

Rosetta — One with a 'rosette' coat pattern, i.e. with light spots in darker circles, as in the Bengal breed.

Ruffles — For one with a ruff, or circle of a different colour fur, around its neck.

Santa — After who else but Santa *Claws*, and perhaps for a red-and-white cat the colour of Father Christmas's coat.

Satin — A slinky variety.

Shaggy — For a long-haired type.

Shrimp — A tiny little albino with pink points?

Skipper — A cat that skips, or for a blue marine type.

Slim — For a thin one.

Slinx — A lissom cat that slinks around.

Smarties — For a Persian Odd-eyed White?

Smiler — After *Smilodon*, the best-known of the sabre-tooth tiger fossils. For a sabre-toothed puss or just one with a Cheshire-cat grin?

Snagglepuss — Another feline creation from the studios of Hanna-Barbera, this genial but calamitous lion featured in the *Huckleberry Hound Show* and had such catchphrases as 'Heavens to Murgatroyd' and 'Exit, Stage Left'. A snag tooth is a broken or protruding one, so perhaps again for a large-toothed cat. (**Murgatroyd**)

Spades — For a *spayed* cat as black as the ace of spades?

Spats — 'Spats' is the shortened version of 'spatterdashes', originally long leather leggings designed to protect footwear from mud, but later stylish white coverings for shoes, especially in the 1920s. Hence a good name for a cat with white paws.

Specs/Spex — An alternative name for a ring-eyed type.

Spike — A comic Goon of a cat or one with sharp claws.

Sprog — Slang for a baby.

Squinancy — A pink-point pussy, after the plant.

Stubbs — For one with a stubby tail.

Studs — A really macho tom, probably also with spots or studs in its fur colouring.

Svengali — For a cat with mesmerizing eyes.

Tamberlaine/Byron — For lame cats.

Tangles — A cat with matted fur or one that's always in a tangle.

Tatters — A scruffy moggy.

Teasy — A prickly puss, after the teasel plant.

Thorny/Thornton — A spiky customer or a delicious brown, after the chocolates.

Titfer — A cat with a hat ('Tit for tat' is rhyming slang for 'hat').

Tramp — A streetwise mongrel.

Trike — A three-legged cat?

Tuck — After Friar Tuck, the fat man in Robin Hood's gang — for a jolly, fat brown type.

Tufty — Many cats have lynx-like tufted ears.

Tulip — One with a chewed lip? Also the Persian word for 'turban' so perhaps for one with a hat.

Turpin — A masked desperado, after highwayman Dick Turpin.

Ursula — Latin for 'little bear'.

Vinny/Vincent — For a one-eared mog, after Vincent van Gogh.

Walrus — An unfortunately savage cat with large whiskers — as the saying goes: your walrus hurt the one you love!

Wedgie — For any variety with a wedge-shaped head.

Wellington — A distinguished cat with a big nose and large boots...

Wickets — For a three-legged type.

Wiscus — A cat owned by T. S. Eliot, but for any heavily whiskered puss.

Woodruff — For a cat with a brown ruff?

Zipper/Zippo/Zips — For a neutered cat, after the scar pattern left from its op? 'Zippo' is also the US word for 'nothing'...

Zits — A spotty pussy.

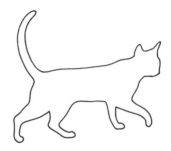

COMICAL
CATS

Early cat humour

For some reason humorous artists seem to delight in portraying cats. Indeed, one of the earliest comic drawings must be Wenceslaus Hollar's picture of a cat receiving a deputation of rats (Hollar also did a magnificent engraving of the Grand Duke of Muscovy's cat in 1663). And the Japanese artist Kuniyoshi (1798-1861) published lots of comic prints featuring felines, including a series of caricatures of actors drawn as cats in full colour, each portrait framed in a collar with a bell on it. Not to be forgotten, too, are the superb drawings by Grandville illustrating Balzac's satirical novel *Peines de coeur d'une chatte Anglaise* in which **Minette**, who is married to a stuffy English aristocrat cat, has an affair with **Brisquet** (an attaché at the French Embassy), is discovered, divorced and finds her lover murdered. (*Wenceslaus, Kuniyoshi, Grandville/Granville*)

The silent miaow

There have been many animated cat cartoons over the years but the great grandpappy of them all is **Felix** the Cat. An enormous success in the 1920s and a major innovation in the world of animation, the saucer-eyed black-and-white moggy was created by Pat Sullivan in the USA and was originally called Tom. However, though the brave little hero had numerous adventures and escaped all kinds of perils using his wit and feline cunning — sometimes even by removing his tail! — he never said a word. The only dialogue associated with him was a song, 'Felix

Kept on Walking', played in the theatres where the films were shown. Unassailable in the era of silent comedy, Felix and his creator gradually slipped from the limelight as Sullivan held out against the advent of sound cinema, believing the investment to be too great. An early competitor called Walt Disney gambled on the future and the rest, as they say, is history. (**Pat**, **Walt**)

Disney cats

Cats appear in many Disney cartoons but perhaps the best known are those that star in *The Aristocats* (1970). The main protagonists are an alleycat named **Thomas O'Malley** and an elegant Parisian *chatte* by the name of **Duchess** who speaks with the voice of Eva Gabor. Stranded in the French countryside with her three kittens, **Marie**, **Toulouse** and **Berlioz**, Duchess is befriended by O'Malley and with his help they manage to find their way back to Paris and happiness, having many adventures and singing memorable Disney melodies en route.

A cartoon Oscar cat

Of the many cartoon cat-and-mouse films that have appeared, from **Mr Jinx** and Pixie and Dixie to **Herman** and Katnip and from **Percy** and Little Roquefort to **Oil Can Harry** and Mightymouse, perhaps the best-known are the **Tom** and Jerry shorts made by William Hanna and Joseph Barbera for MGM. The first one appeared in 1939 and was an instant success. The team then went on to win four Oscars in a row from 1943 to 1946, beginning with *Yankee Doodle Mouse*, and notched up a further three in 1948, 1951 and 1952, breaking Disney's monopoly of the awards in this field. When Hanna and Barbera left MGM in 1957 to set up their own studio, Chuck Jones produced a series and another was made in Czechoslovakia by Gene Deitch. However, Hanna and Barbera returned to the characters in 1976 and made a number of cartoons for TV but

they lacked the quality of the original series. It is perhaps ironical to note that sound cinema, which contributed to the demise of Felix the Cat, should have worked so much in Tom and Jerry's favour — it must be the background crashes, bangs and scoldings from the black housekeeper that add to the films' attraction, as the cat and mouse themselves never utter a word. (*Hanna*, *Katnip*, *Chuck*)

Fritz, the X-rated cat

The 'underground' cartoonist Robert Crumb, creator of **Fritz the Cat**, was once described by *Time* magazine as an 'American Hogarth' who'd brought back the vigour and eroticism of the Regency period to graphic art. However, though acclaimed by the critics, it appeared that such sexual explicitness and violence was not to the prudish censor's taste, and when an animated feature was made in 1972, based on Crumb's original magazine-strip creation, it had the dubious honour of being the first ever cartoon film to receive an X certificate.

Directed by Ralph Bakshi and produced by Steve Krantz, the film follows the adventures of the foul-mouthed streetwise ginger tom — based originally on Crumb's own cat **Fred** — across America in a riot of bathtub orgies, bar-room brawls and confrontations with the police (depicted as pigs). From its first screening it was an instant hit and is now regarded as an animation classic, but Crumb himself benefited little from his creation's success, having sold the rights for a lump sum. And in a final act of pique he put paid to Fritz's future by killing him off in a magazine strip later the same year — in appropriate lowlife manner he was murdered by a jilted female ostrich armed with an icepick.

The Boss Cat

There have been a number of feline stars on the small screen, from **Courageous** Cat to **Riff-Raff** and from **Heathcliff** to **James** the Cat, but the most popular made-for-TV series is still *Top Cat* with its wisecracking hero **TC**, as he likes to be known. Owing something to the style of *Sergeant Bilko* (and indeed the voice of the fat blue cat **Benny the Ball** is supplied by a *Bilko* actor) the cartoons revolve around the activities of Top Cat and his cronies such as **Fancy**, **Choo-Choo** and the dull-witted **Brain** in an alley full of garbage cans. In their constant battle for survival their one antagonist is Police Officer Dibble who is constantly outwitted by the cunning TC and his company of feline felons. All the animals talk and walk on two feet and TC himself wears a waistcoat and a straw boater through which his ears protrude. First shown in 1961 and produced by Hanna-Barbera, the series is still as successful as ever. (**Bilko**, **Dibble**)

Cat megastar

The bestselling cartoon strip character of all time (now surpassing even Snoopy — who is, after all, a mere dog, when all is said and done) is undoubtedly Jim Davis's fat ginger cat, **Garfield**. Created in 1977 as a newspaper strip, the character quickly became tremendously popular, and as a measure of his success, three Garfield collections appeared on the *New York Times* bestseller list at the same time in 1982 — a feat unrivalled by any author. And the fame of the pasta-chomping tom with the heavy-lidded eyes continues apace. As well as appearing in his own TV series, a vast international merchandising empire now features his image, philosophy and wisecracks embossed on countless products from cups to nappies — and you can now even buy own-brand Garfield lasagne!

The puddy tat

Warner Brothers' hugely popular scrawny cat, **Sylvester**, first appeared in *A Tale of Two Kitties* in 1942, though in the early films he was called **Thomas**. The voice of the lisping, long-suffering black-and-white tom with the red nose was supplied

by Mel Blanc who also did that of his never-conquered prey, Tweetie Pie the canary, whose cry of 'I taut I taw a puddy tat' is now so familiar. Sylvester's own favourite phrase, encapsulating a lifetime of frustration, was 'Sufferin' succotash!', sprayed out for nearly two decades during which the series notched up a brace of Academy awards (1947 and 1957) under directors Fritz Freleng, Chuck Jones and Robert McKimson. Other movies starring the ill-fated cat featured Speedy Gonzalez 'the fastest mouse in all Mexico', Porky Pig and a kangaroo named Hoppy. (**Warner, *Mel***)

PERSONALITIES

Abacus — A calculating cat (**Calculus** Cat features in the Underground comics of Hunt Emerson).

Ace — For a really ace cat.

Ackemma — An early-morning type (Service slang for 'a.m.').

Alan — From the Celtic meaning 'in tune' — for a melodious moggy, especially a Manx or 'Spanish' cat. (**Catalan**)

Alexis — A name of Greek origin meaning 'helper'.

Ali — From Tin Pan Alley, for a musical cat that always has his head in a tin! Ali is also an Arabic name meaning 'lion of God'.

Almeric — From the Teutonic for 'energetic'.

Amanda — Latin for 'lovable' — for a lovable cat.

Antonia — A good name for a much-treasured or indeed very expensive type — the name comes from the Latin for 'priceless'.

Arvak — From the Norse for 'early waker' — an alarm-call cat.

Augustus/Julius/Tiberius/Nero — All good imperial names. Also **Galba**, **Otho**, **Vitellius**, **Vespasian**, **Titus** and **Domitian**.

Ballou/Barbarella — After Cat Ballou, the feisty Wild West lady played by Jane Fonda in the film of the same name, and the eponymous beautiful sci-fi sex kitten in another movie starring Ms Fonda. (*Jane*)

Basket — One that's always in its basket or a slightly mad puss, a basket case?

Baudelaire — For a particularly poetic puss, after the French poet who wrote a number of verses to cats in his collection *Les Fleurs du Mal*.

Beelzebub — The satanic Beelzebub gets his name from the Hebrew for 'lord of the flies', so for a bluebottle-chasing type?

Betjeman — A cat that's 'summoned by bells', after the title of a book by the poet.

Big Brother — A cat that's always watching you! After the character in George Orwell's *Nineteen Eighty-Four*.

Bingo — A little old lady's cry of delight?

Bloater — A pig of a fish-eater?

Bob — For a real wild cat, or one that sings a lot, after 'bobcat' and Bing Crosbie's brother Bob's jazz band known as the Bob-cats. (*Bing*)

Bojangles — A musical cat.

Bonzo/Bonzer — 'Bonzer' is Australian slang for 'excellent'. Perhaps too for a retriever cat that thinks it's a dog?

Boogie — For a dancer.

Botham — A great all-rounder...

Brains — A particularly bright, or very stupid cat.

Brigitte — After Brigitte Bardot, the original sex-kitten. (*Bardot*)

Brock — For a cat that's always badgering you.

Buck — For a male.

Buffalo Bill — A real humdinger of a Wild West show cat, after Buffalo Bill Cody (1846-1917) — particularly for long-haired varieties.

Bugatti — For a cat with a classy chassis that can really move.

Busby — Not after the British telephone service cartoon bird but the bearskin hat worn by guardsmen at Buckingham Palace and elsewhere — or are they cats that they wear on their heads?

Bussy — 'Buss' is an archaic word for a kiss — for a bussy pussy.

Buster — For an inscrutable stone-face cat with a great sense of humour and highly athletic, after its silent-movie namesake who performed all his own stunts...Buster Kitten?

Buzz — For a cat that always seems to be high up — on the roof, in a tree — after astronaut Edwin 'Buzz' Aldrin, the second man to set foot on the moon on 20 July 1969. Or for a cat with a very loud purr. (*Edwin*)

Calliope — Meaning 'beautiful voice'. Calliope was one of the Muses.

Caruso — For a cat that sings a lot, and also a black cat with green eyes owned by the writer and critic Edmund Gosse (1849-1928).

Champion — So why should horses get all the good names? What about Champion the Wonder Cat? (You wonder where he is, what he's doing, is he OK?)

Chow/Ciao — For one that likes its food or, alternatively, with the Italian spelling, one that's always going off on its own...

Claude/Claud — For a cat that claws a lot.

Clemenceau — The great French statesman Georges Clemenceau (1841-1929), twice prime minister of France and negotiator of the Treaty of Versailles, was known as 'the Tiger' — for a diplomatic but tough type.

Clignette — A female cat that winks (*cligner* is French for 'to wink').

Clint — A mean, slit-eyed type that has a habit of walking slowly. For a cat that just goes ahead and makes your day!

Constance/Connie — A solid name for a dependable puss, or for one that constantly wants food. Or for one who particularly likes gardeners? (After Lady Constance Chatterley in Lawrence's novel.) (*Lady Chatterley*)

Coventry — For a silent type that goes off by itself?

Dan/Danny — A desperate cat, after the cartoon character. Or after the song 'Danny Boy' for whom 'the pipes, the pipes are calling', for a cat that sits on radiators!

Dash — For a cat that dashes about the place.

Désirée — A desirable female.

Dhobi — A cat that's always washing itself (from the Indian name for a washerwoman).

Diddler — After the fictional scrounger, Jeremy Diddler. (*Jeremy*)

Dippy — For an eccentric or crazy type.

Dither — A cat that sits on the fence.

Dizzy — A flighty or confused moggy.

Dodger — A thieving cat, after Dickens's the Artful Dodger, or for a crafty type after the comic character, Roger the Dodger.

Dodo — From the Portuguese meaning 'stupid', or for any cat that is determined to be the last of its kind.

Doolittle/Dolittle — For a lazy cat, or for one who talks to animals (after Dr Dolittle).

Doughty — A hardy and resolute type. Or perhaps for an adventurous one, after the explorer Charles Doughty.

Dudley — After 'Cuddly' Dudley Moore, internationally renowned comic actor and musician. For a small, slightly lunatic but very cuddly cat.

Dutch — For a dear old duchess of a puss…

Duvet — A cat that always seems to be on the bed!

Egeria — A wise-counselling nymph.

Eleanor — After Eleanor Rigby who sat by a window in the Beatles song, and also after Eleanor Coade for whom the Coade Lion on Westminster Bridge is named (it's made of Coade stone). (**Rigby**)

Elfa — An elfa-leather cat!

Everest — A cat that's always asleep.

Excelsior — Meaning 'excellent'.

Fairy/Fay — A spritely feline.

Flapdoodle — A cat that talks nonsense.

Floyd — Either for a rather spaced-out cat (after the pop group Pink Floyd) or for one that dotes on fish (after TV gastronaut Keith Floyd who rocketed to fame with the programme *Floyd on Fish*). (**Keith**)

Ford — A cat that likes to travel in cars and after Ford Madox Ford who wrote the poem 'The Cat in the House'. (See also *A Cat Miscellany*.)

Fusspot — A fussy pussy.

Gannet — A food-fanatic feline.

Ganos — Greek for 'joy'.

Garbo/Howard — For cats that want to be alone, after Greta Garbo and Howard Hughes. (**Greta, Hughes**)

Gatsby — For a *great* cat.

Gavroche — The street-arab in Hugo's *Les Misérables*.

Gideon — The destroyer (Hebrew).

Glossy — A sleek, shining example.

Gobbo — The clown in *The Merchant of Venice*.

Godot — A cat you always have to wait for...

Governor — He's the boss.

Harpo — A silent type, after Harpo Marx.

Hawkeye — He never misses a thing.

Henrietta/Henriette — For a cat that doesn't lose its head, after Henrietta Maria, whose husband, Charles I of England, did. Also after the great French painter of cats, Madame Henriette Ronner. (**Maria**)

Hinse — After Hinse of Hinsefield, the cat owned by Sir Walter Scott (see *Cats of the Famous*), but also for any moggy that has a habit of giving you hints that it is hungry, wants to go out etc.

Homer — A home-loving cat.

Hubbard — For a cupboard-love cat, after Old Mother Hubbard who went to the cupboard in the nursery rhyme.

Humpty-Dumpty — For a cat that sits on walls.

Hunter — A hunting type.

Hush — A remarkably quiet cat.

Ignatius — A fiery cat.

Jack/Jacko — For a Jack-the-lad cat that's always chasing the birds! Also after Wacko Jacko, pop star Michael Jackson, for one not sure if he's black or white? (And see *Blacks and Black-and-Whites*.)

Jack Sprat — For a cat that will eat no fat, after the nursery rhyme.

Jake — Australian slang for 'all right' or 'satisfactory', or from Jacob which in Hebrew means 'one who supplants' — know the feeling?

Jankers — For a housebound cat, after the RAF slang usage.

Jim — A real Gentleman Jim type, or alternatively for a lucky cat, after Kingsley Amis's character in the novel *Lucky Jim*. (**Kingsley**)

Jingles — What else would you call him after 'belling the cat'?

Johnson — After Pussy Foot Johnson, chief architect of Prohibition in the USA — for a strict cat.

Jonah — A bit of a jinx, this one...

Josh — To josh is to tease.

Kent/Clark — After Clark Kent, for a Supercat!

Kester — A variant of Kit.

Kilroy — He always gets there first...

Kipper — For a brown or smoky cat that's always sleeping?

Kitson — For a sonofabitch cat?

Kitty — A common cat-call. For a paper tiger or after Christopher Catt who founded the Kit-cat Club.

Lesley — After Lesley Anne Ivory, cat portraitist extraordinaire and her many feline friends, especially **Agneatha** and her children **Bracken**, **Bramble** and **Biggles**.

Livingstone — You'll always find him eventually.

Loopy — A crazy cat.

Lothario — A bit of a libertine...

Mae — A cat that's always on the bed and seems to be saying 'Come up and see me some time', after Mae West. Also the name of one that lived in London's Connaught Theatre.

Maestro — The master!

Maigret — An investigative French (long-haired) cat.

Malvolio — For an ill-willed type and after the steward in *Twelfth Night*.

Matins — For an early riser.

Merlin — A real wizard cat.

Micawber — A cat that's always waiting for something to turn up — after the Dickens character.

Mimi — An onomatopoeic name of a mewing moggy but also the cat in Huysmans's book *En Rade*, based on one of his own cats known as Barre-en-Rouille. The author himself has been described as being both in manner and appearance like a cat, so Huysmans might be another good name. (*Huysmans*)

Minx — A flirtatious feline.

Mischief — Always up to no good.

Molly — For a cuddly cat, from 'molly-coddle'; or for a tough female, as in 1920s US gangster jargon 'gun-moll'. (See also *Classical and Classy Cats.*)

Monkey — A real monkey...

Monty — Montgomery, Monty Python, Monty Sunshine Jazz Band — take your pick.

Morgan — If male, for a racy cat after the famous sports car; or a cat that looks like it might once have been a pirate on the high seas, after T.S. Eliot's Cat Morgan that is 'com-mission-aire' at publishers Faber & Faber. If female, then named for Morgan le Fay, Queen of Avalon and half-sister of King Arthur.

Morpheus/Morph — The Greek god of sleep and dreams, for a dozy type.

Moth — One that always flies by night (there is an actual species called a puss moth). And also after François de la Mothe le Vayer (1588-1672) who wrote a famous epitaph on a cat. (*François*)

Mumbles — Is she talking or is it just a purr?

Murr — Another miaowing or purring name for a cat and also one that occurs in the writings of E. T. A. Hoffman whose fantasy stories inspired Offenbach's *Tales of Hoffman*. Not only does his cat appear in a number of stories, but in one, 'Murr the Cat and his Views on Life', is allegedly part-author. For a particularly literary feline that is rather *demure*!

Natch — A really natural cat.

Nelly — For a cat that likes to be near streams, after the song 'Nelly Dean'.

Nibbles — A nibbling cat.

Nona — For a cat with all nine lives still.

Oedipus — A puss with parental problems...

Oliver — For a cat that always seems to ask for more, after Charles Dickens's character.

Olympuss — For one that deserves a medal.

Omaha — Omaha is the female star of the strip-cartoon series, 'Omaha the Cat Dancer' by Reed Waller and Kate Worley, featuring the trials and tribulations of a nightclub striptease cat — perhaps for a sexy dancing queen? (**Reed, Kate**)

Orion — The mighty hunter.

Orpheus — The poetic lyre-player of Greek myth — for a lyrical type.

Oscar — After Oscar Wilde, who was described by Max Beerbohm as having a 'cat-like tread', but also for any cat that deserves an Academy Award.

Pansy — Not for a *poofy* cat but for a thinker (the plant is named from *pensée*, French for 'thought').

Parker — After Lady Penelope's chauffeur in TV's *Thunderbirds*. (**Penelope**)

Pasha — An oriental governor.

Passepartout — For a cat that seems to be everywhere, from Fogg's companion in Jules Verne's *Around the World in Eighty Days* and the French word meaning a skeleton key.

Pawky — A paw-ky cat — one with a dry wit.

Peerless — A peerless puss.

Percy — Much better-sounding than 'pussy' and also the name of the cat villain in the *Little Roquefort* cartoon series as well as the one immortalized in David Hockney's famous painting *Mr and Mrs Clark and Percy*.

Piers — For a cat with a habit of peering at you?

Pipemma — A late-night type (Service slang for 'p.m.').

Pizzazz — 'An attractive combination of energy and style; sparkle, vitality and glamour' (*Collins Dictionary*) — name that cat!

Pogo — For a remarkably bouncy cat.

Polly — Many cats seem to want to sit on your shoulder like Long John Silver's parrot in R.L. Stevenson's *Treasure Island*, so why not Polly? (See also *Tortoiseshells, Particolours and Mongrels*.)

Pongo — Another name for a gorilla, and slang for a soldier — perhaps also for a smelly cat?

Poppy — A pretty name for a little flower.

Portnoy — A cat that's always playing with its nether parts? After the Philip Roth character.

Pounce — An energetic cat (or **NRG**?).

Presto — Suddenly, hey presto! — he's there.

Puck — An Old Norse word meaning a mischievous sprite, so highly appropriate for a naughty cat or kitten — a real hobgoblin, as depicted by Shakespeare in *A Midsummer Night's Dream*.

Raffles — After the great cat burglar or amateur cracksman invented by E.W. Hornung — for a cat on a hot tin roof?

Rambo — For a very tough, or alternatively a very weedy cat, after the movie character played by Sylvester Stallone.

Rascal/Rebel — A little tearaway.

Reilly — For a cat that lives the luxurious 'life of Reilly'.

Rip Van Winkle — For a dozy cat, after the story of a man who just seems to keep on sleeping, by Washington Irving. (**Washington**)

Robson — For a literary cat of considerable refinement, after the publisher of this book.

Rocket — A streak of a cat.

Rossini — For a cat that caterwauls a lot, after the composer who wrote the hilarious duet for two cats.

Rover — One that's always on the move.

Rummy — For a cat that's a bit of a card...

Rumpuscat — The Great Rumpuscat in Eliot's *Old Possum's Book of Practical Cats* appears at the end of 'The Awefull Battle of the Pekes and the Pollicles' and scattered the lot.

With eyes like fireballs, amazing jaws 'You never saw anything fiercer or hairier' — for a real old bruiser.

Rum Tum Tugger — After Eliot's Curious Cat that always wants to be out when you have let him in, always wants meat when you give him fish and vice-versa — a real contrary type, 'For he will do/As he do do/And there's no doing anything about it!'

Sanura — The Swahili word for 'like a kitten'.

Scamp — For a scalliwag.

Séraphita — The Seraphs were the highest order of angels in the celestial hierarchy, so this was an appropriate name for one of Theóphile Gautier's many female cats, described in *Le Ménagerie Intime* as being 'of a dreamy disposition …delighted in perfumes…walked upon the dressing-table among the scent bottles, smelling the stoppers'. For a discerning, fragrant female.

Sherpa/Hillary/Tenzing — For a cat that always seems to be climbing over everything, after the conquerors of Everest, Sir Edmund Hillary and his Sherpa guide, Tenzing Norgay.

Simon — For a rather simple cat, or alternatively for a brave one, after Simon the cat VC (see *Top Cats*).

Simpson —A rather refined type — after the Piccadilly store.

Sisyphus — For a cat that likes playing with balls, after the Greek king condemned to roll a rock up a hill for eternity.

Snapdragon/Snapper — A cat with bite.

Solitaire — For a jewel of a cat that likes to play by itself.

Sophie — A nice soft name from the Greek for 'wisdom', and after a 1st-century Christian martyr, St Sophia — for a cat that sits on the sofa?

Søren — After Søren Kierkegaard, for a philosophical type that's often in the churchyard (*kierkegaard* is Danish for 'churchyard').

Spencer — For a cat that never leaves marks!

Spitfire — A hard-to-handle cat.

Stalky — One that stalks a lot.

Sultan/Sultana — An oriental ruler. Perhaps also for a brown female, after the dried grapes?

Tantivy — A full-speed-ahead cat.

Tarot — Look into its eyes and see the future...

Teraph — A teraph was a small household god amongst ancient Semitic peoples.

Theakston — For an 'Old Peculiar' cat, after the famous Yorkshire beer.

Toots/Tootsie — US word for 'darling' or 'sweetheart'.

Tortrix — From the Latin word for 'twister'.

Towser — A cat that tears at things (see also *Record-Breaking Cats*).

Triton — For a cat that tries it on...

Turps — For a terpsichorean or dancing type.

Twinkle/Twinkletoes — A light-footed puss — it is also a fact that cats walk on their toes, unlike humans.

Twitch — A lot of cats do this...

Ulysses/Odysseus/Columbus/Vasco — Names for a wandering, explorer type.

Valentino — The ultimate romantic lover cat.

Vespers — An evening ves-puss.

Vesta — Roman goddess of the hearth, which is where a cat loves to be.

Vox — Latin for 'voice'.

Walker — Like Felix, he just keeps on walking.

Walton — The compleat angler cat — a great fisherman or one that's always angling for things?

Wamba — After the jester in Scott's *Ivanhoe*. (*Scott*)

Webster — For a cat that likes books, after the famous US dictionary. Also after the cat described in P. G. Wodehouse's story. (*Wodehouse*)

Whisper — A softly purring puss?

Wilco — RAF slang for 'will cooperate' — a cooperative feline.

Willoughby — The egoist in Meredith's book. (**Meredith**)

Wistaria — A popular climbing type.

Wogan — For a cat that's never off the TV!

Yeoman — A beef-eating cat.

Zero — One that moves like lightning when dinner appears, or a particularly fiendish oriental fighting cat (after the Mitsubishi Zero fighter plane of World War II). (**Mitsubishi**)

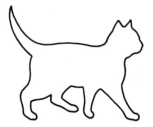

A CAT
MISCELLANY

A lucky cat-lick

The British Labour statesman, Ramsay MacDonald, is reputed to have once said that his success in life dated from an encounter with a black cat in a London post office. This clever creature had been trained to lick stamps and when as a young man MacDonald employed its services to stick the appropriate amount on a letter it changed his life. For the envelope contained an article he was sending to *The Times*. To his delight the article was accepted and MacDonald's career had begun in earnest. Who says philately gets you nowhere! (**Ramsay, MacDonald**)

Junkie cats

It hardly seems possible that such a self-possessed and demure creature as the domestic cat could be a victim of drug-taking, but that is exactly what modern scientists believe happens when they encounter catnip, valerian and certain other garden herbs. Apparently they are unaffected until the age of three months, but thereafter as many as half of all cats (including, believe it or not, lions!) are susceptible to the plants and get a high off their perfume. By all accounts they seem to experience some form of inner delight or ecstasy and roll around, leap in the air, purr, miaow and rub their heads on the leaves in a most unbecoming manner. However, there is no need to call out the RSPCA to prevent hordes of crazed psychedelic cats from tottering through your flowerbeds in search of the magic weed

as the effect only lasts about ten minutes or so, after which the animals revert to their sober, respectable selves.

Vampire cats

According to some biblical traditions, Adam's *original* wife was Lilith who, refusing to honour and obey her lord and master, flew off, turned into a vampire and assumed the form of a large black cat whose favourite prey was new-born babies — which may account for some people's fear of cats in the nursery.

The vampire-cat theme recurs in the Japanese legend of the Prince of Hizen whose lover O Toyo is killed one night by a large cat which leaps at her throat, then buries the body and assumes her form. Suspecting nothing the Prince continues to meet the vampire each night until he becomes mortally ill through loss of blood. Fearing for his life, a watch is kept on him round the clock but the guards are mesmerized by the cat-woman's beauty until one, Ito Soda, keeps himself alert by stabbing his arm and discovers what is happening. Attempting to kill the vampire, he is thwarted when she reverts to the form of a cat and escapes into the mountains. However, when the Prince recovers, he sends his hunters out to kill the creature and rewards Ito Soda handsomely. (**Lilith**, **Hizen**)

Pussy mummies

The Egyptians were so fond of their cats that when they died they were embalmed and mummified with as much care — if not more — than their human counterparts. Indeed, some temple cats, which were regarded as living symbols of the great Bast herself, had highly ornamented caskets and casings moulded out of bronze.

The major cat-burial centres were situated at Thebes, Speos Artemidos, Bubastis etc. — cities dedicated to the worship of Bast — and mummified moggies from all over Egypt were sent to such sacred places for interment. In the nineteenth cen-

tury one of these enormous burial chambers was discovered at Beni Hasan where literally hundreds of thousands of miniature corpses were found laid out in carefully ordered rows on shelves. Sadly, many were burnt by locals or sold to tourists, but the worst was yet to come. So great were the numbers involved that one enterprising tradesman hit on the idea of grinding them up and selling them as manure. Accordingly, 180,000 of the cloth-wrapped cats were shipped to Liverpool and auctioned off at £3 13s 4d a ton. To add insult to injury the insensitive auctioneer even used one of the lovingly embalmed bodies as a gavel! To think that creatures so greatly revered in their lifetimes should come to such an inglorious end...

Cats at war

No less than 500,000 stout patriotic cats were officially employed by the British forces in World War I. Defying creeping barrages and the Flanders mud they heroically served their country, keeping down rats, mice and other pests in the trenches. One of their less enjoyable additional duties was to alert the troops to the advance of clouds of poison gas, and many thousands more men would have succumbed to this evil weapon of war if it hadn't been for the cats' valiant sacrifice.

The use of cats in gas warfare in fact has a more ancient history, for as far back as the 16th century Christopher of Habsburg invented a system whereby cats carrying bottles of poisonous vapours strapped to their backs would be released at an enemy, spreading the noxious fumes behind them as they went. A drawing of this device, looking not unlike a feline doodlebug rocket, exists in a manuscript in Strasburg, but the lack of evidence to support its actual employment in battle seems to attest to the unwillingness of the Renaissance cat to succumb to such indignity.

In 1941 the British Minister of Food declared that all cats 'engaged in work of national importance' were to receive an official powdered milk ration. However, in order to qualify they had to be employed in keeping down vermin in stores containing at least 250 tons of food or animal foodstuffs. And such was the cat's worth in this role that in 1948 the USA mounted a Cats for Europe campaign — literally thousands of Yankee moggies were shipped to France to protect valuable stores from rats and mice.

But perhaps the most bizarre cat war story concerns a black cat donated by a Pennsylvanian family which was reputedly flown to England and then over Europe as a 'special envoy'. Its mission? To cross Hitler's path and bring him bad luck! (Maybe they really meant it to cross Churchill's path to bring him *good* luck...)

Deaf cats

According to medical testimony, first published in Darwin's *Origin of Species* in the last century, most blue-eyed cats are virtually stone deaf — which probably accounts for the painful atonality of the average moggy troubadour. However, azure-eyed cat-owners need not despair. For according to another popular theory, to know what a cat is thinking all you need do is hold its paw in your hand for a while — though it is not explained if this is some kind of thought-transference, the exchange of a mystical cat masonic handshake, or a feline variety of braille. Perhaps a hearing aid would be simpler?

Music-hall moggies

George Robey, the celebrated Victorian British music-hall entertainer, once spent a month of intensive work training 12 cats to appear with him in a stage act. After considerable effort, and not without many sleepless nights worrying about whether they'd be ready in time, Robey finally assembled the cats on stage for their big premiére. All had been carefully washed, powdered and combed and to his great relief each sat on its appointed chair as arranged. However, as the curtain rose on

the comedian and his feline friends a member of the audience went 'pthisst!' and the panicked cats leapt off their chairs and disappeared without trace. Robey was devastated but the audience, thinking it all a deliberate leg-pull, loved it and burst into laughter and spontaneous applause. Not one to miss an opportunity, Robey immediately regained his composure and played up to the crowd, taking bows and turning what could have been a disaster into one of his greatest successes. (*Robey*)

The revenge of Bast

The influential American dancer and choreographer, Isadora Duncan, positively despised cats and actively persecuted them. This may have been partly due to the fact that her next-door neighbour in Neuilly, France, was a countess who had given over her house as a sanctuary for stray moggies. However, Duncan's dislike of the animals was excessive and whenever one of the cats was found in her garden she would order her servants to hunt it down and drown it. The Countess often remonstrated but to no avail and once even found a dead stray hanging from a cord over the party wall. But perhaps Ms Duncan's cruelty didn't go unpunished after all, for both her children were drowned in the Seine during her lifetime and, as a final ironic twist, the great dancer herself was killed by strangulation when her long flowing scarf caught in the wheels of a car. (*Isadora*)

The motorized purr

The American motor manufacturer Henry Ford is remembered as the author of a number of sayings, including 'History is bunk' and reaches godlike stature in Aldous Huxley's novel *Brave New World* where time itself is dated from 'the Year of Our Ford'. However, he also had opinions on cats and when asked if he'd like to own one replied: 'Do you know why I

should like a cat of my very own? Its pleasant purring would remind me of the products of my works. I should imagine myself listening to the distant purring of my motors, and in the cat I should love the purring of my cars, and in the cars I should hear the purring of my cat.'

This fantasy actually became unhappy reality in September 1983 when an eight-year-old black female called **Buttons** accidentally set the record for the greatest distance travelled by a cat under the bonnet of a car. Setting off on a business trip from Great Yarmouth in Norfolk the driver didn't discover the stowaway until he stopped at a service station in Newcastle six hours and 300 miles later. The hot and oily cat was cleaned up and fed, and on arrival at the traveller's destination in Aberdeen an airline heard of her adventure and flew her back to Norwich free, where she was reunited with her owner, the car driver's next-door neighbour.

Lobby cats

Some hotels seem to be almost as famous for their feline members of staff as for their cuisine and accommodation. The example of **Hamlet** at the Algonquin in New York is a case in point, and **Whisky** and **Soda** were two famous cats that lived in the Stafford Hotel in London's Mayfair. The Savoy goes one stage further by having a perennial cat, **Kaspar**. Carved out of wood by Basil Ionides and in situ since 1916 he is reputedly placed in the 13th seat at any gathering of over a dozen people to banish ill-luck. (*Basil, Ionides*)

Cats in fish shock

In 1938 four cats were employed to patrol the aquarium at New York's Zoo and keep down the rats. For some time they performed their duties admirably but one day Dr Coates, the head keeper, discovered that one of the rare fish had been stolen from the tank and, guessing who the culprits were, decided to teach

the cats a lesson. Removing the feline felons from the scene of the crime, he fished several electric eels from the aquarium and laid them out carefully on the floor next to the tank. He then let the cats in. The four animals instantly pounced on the squirming eels but leapt back in alarm when they received a number of powerful shocks as the fish defended themselves. Suitably chastised, the four guards were later returned to their patrol and from that day onwards no fish ever went missing again!

Cuisine for cats

It is well-known that Dr Johnson fed his great cat **Hodge** on oysters but cats have also been recorded as eating, with apparent relish, all manner of oddities. The Canadian writer Francis Dickie owned a black tomcat that happily munched uncooked bread dough, tinned beans, macaroni cheese and strawberry shortcake and was not averse to chomping a cigar if one was left around! But the cat that really must take the biscuit for dietary diversity was Lafcadio Hearn's little red kitten which apparently ate 'beefsteak and cockroaches, caterpillars and fish, chicken and butterflies, mosquito hawks and roast mutton, hash and tumblebugs, beetles and pigs' feet, crabs and spiders, moths and poached eggs, oysters and earthworms, ham and mice, rats and rice pudding — until its belly became a realization of Noah's Ark'.

However, when it comes to the choicest moggie menus, aid is at hand in the form of Richard Graham's *Cuisine for Cats*. Stuck at home with their female Abyssinian while his wife earnt a crust as a ballet dancer, Richard thought it would make sense to cook both for himself and the discerning **Rifan Sabishi**. The resulting book describes his gastronomic adventures, from fish soup and taramasalata to stuffed carp and kedgeree and from kosher katfood to Manx kippers (they have no tails...). And for a finale he even makes recommendations for weightwatching and cat dinner parties! (*Dickie*, *Lafcadio*, *Graham*)

A cuckoo kitten

In Gilbert White's *Natural History of Selborne* the author describes in letter XXXIV how a friend found a leveret and fed it milk from a spoon. One day it went missing at about the same time that their cat kittened. They duly killed and buried the kittens and assumed that the leveret had been eaten by a dog until one evening the cat appeared on the lawn, followed by the leveret which she had suckled on her own milk! That a carnivorous animal should raise one of its natural prey in such a way having lost its own kittens is quite remarkable, though as White says: 'it is not one whit more marvellous that Romulus and Remus...should be nursed by a she-wolf, than that a poor sucking leveret should be fostered and cherished by a bloody grimalkin'.

However, this example is far from unusual, and cases have even been recorded, both in Britain and the USA, of cats raising chickens! (*Gilbert*)

Boozing cats

Quite apart from the fictional adventures of Damon Runyon's cat **Lillian**, there have been a number of famous reported cases of tabby topers. In *Novel Notes*, Jerome K. Jerome describes seeing a cat drink from a leaking beer tap until completely sozzled, a similar story being told by Hilaire Belloc; while **Jim**, a pre-war Paddington Station cat, was also well known for his preference for beer to milk as a nightcap. Also on the subject of beer, in the 1920s a grey tomcat kept by the officers of the 52nd Canadian Battalion stationed in England would make a feast of tinned sardines and beer and then walk a tightrope erected in the mess hall!

As to wine, **Peter**, a black cat once employed by London's Savoy Hotel, took a daily glass with the chef and his dog when his morning duties in the cellar were over at 12.30, and con-

tinued to do so for 12 years. In Richard Graham's book *Cuisine for Cats,* Rifan Sabishi was not averse to a saucer of dry rosé wine with her mixed grill. And in a letter to Samuel Butler on Christmas Eve 1879 Miss Savage describes her own cat drinking mulled port and rum punch. Whatever next? Cat cocktail bars? Old toms sitting on park benches swilling meths? A Cats' Temperance League? (**Hilaire**)

A first-class cat

When **Prince Rahula** made a five-day voyage to Panama on the luxury liner *Virginia* a first-class stateroom was booked in his name, complete with silk-upholstered armchairs, a private bathroom etc — all the finest trappings that money could buy. Imagine the surprise of the ships' stewards lined up at attention to receive the 'royal personage' when a cat strode through and took up residence on the silk coverlet of the large bed! (*Virginia*)

Latchkey cats

Sir Isaac Newton is credited with inventing the cat-flap as he is reputed to have cut two different-sized holes in his door to admit his cat and her kitten (why one large one wouldn't have done to admit both must have taxed his genius no end!). And it is certainly true that George Washington sawed out a similar entrance for his feline friends in his Mount Vernon home. However, records seem to suggest that practices on the Continent were somewhat in advance of the rest of the civilized world, for though such *chatières* were common in France throughout the 16th century, they had already begun to disappear by the end of the 17th. Evidently the French, being great cat-lovers, had been 'trained' to open the door for **Minou** and **Minette** by then!

But all these refinements pale into insignificance alongside cats that can not only open internal doors but actually use the front knocker! One of these rare animals, a ginger-and-white

tom called **Billy** from Coventry, used to bang his owners up so often late at night that they even had a shed built in the garden for him to sleep in after his nocturnal perambulations, but to no avail — the only answer was to put padding on the knocker and hope he'd go away! A further variation on this stunt was offered by an ingenious moggy called **Felix** who was photographed in the *Daily Express* returning home through the letterbox — obviously an example of Cat On Delivery! (***Isaac, Newton, Washington***)

Unlucky black cats

One of the unluckiest black cats was **Nigger** who accompanied Captain Scott's last fateful expedition to the Antarctic in 1910. Indeed its nine lives must have been all but used up long before the band of explorers set off — when Captain Oates insisted that the cat be left on board when they set off for the final dash to the Pole a sudden wave washed the poor cat overboard and it was drowned. (***Oates***)

Speedy cats

'Mice in the engine' used to be a common excuse for breakdowns at the famous racing track at Brooklands — rather like 'gremlins' in aircraft of the RAF. As a result, the only animals allowed on the circuit were cats, presumably to catch these fictitious mice.

However, cats played a significant part in the life of former world land-speed record-holder John Cobb. Just before setting off to the USA for his record-breaking run two kittens were born in the cockpit of his monster car. They were named **Inlet** and **Exhaust**!

Cat in the bag

Just before World War II the *Birmingham Post* reported the case of an eight-week-old black kitten being discovered in a French

mailbag at London's Mount Pleasant sorting office. As the bag had travelled from Dunkirk via Dover, the Customs department was alerted, who then contacted the Ministry of Agriculture and Fisheries who in turn recommended quarantine whilst the cat's owners were traced.

Little **Minet**, it was eventually discovered, was in fact a working Parisian post-office cat who had somehow got into the bag by mistake while carrying out his professional duties of hunting *rongeurs* (rodents). After much red tape the cat was eventually released from quarantine and returned to France with its own personalized travel documents and an official licence embossed with a big red seal. One of the conditions on the licence stated that if the cat was lost whilst in the UK the person in charge of it at the time should report the loss immediately by telegram. The suggested message was: 'CATSOPPTIT'!

Tiki the TT cat

Classic British motorcycling ace of the pre-war period, Eric Fernihough, always held that his cats brought him luck. His favourite was **Tiki** who was born three days before his first event in 1923 in which he won no less than six cups, and later every time she gave birth a big win was usually never far away. During her 12-year reign Tiki had between 80 and 90 kittens, making Fernihough one of the most successful TT racers of his day — perhaps this is not surprising when one learns that Tiki was a Manx! But the story doesn't end there, because Fernihough gave one of Tiki's black kittens to a girl he was fond of and she later became his wife — a lucky black cat indeed. (*Eric*)

Famous cat-haters

One has to suppose that the cartoonist Simon Bond, creator of *101 Uses for a Dead Cat* must be an ailurophobe of the highest order, but it doesn't necessarily follow. However, the French

Renaissance poet, Pierre de Ronsard, certainly disliked cats and even wrote verse declaring that no man anywhere hated them more than he. And the otherwise jovial Hilaire Belloc was so disgusted by the feline race that in his essay 'On Them' he couldn't even bring himself to mention the word 'cat' and just referred to 'Them'. But perhaps the most well-known cat-hater was Napoleon who when staying in the palace of Schönbrunn after occupying Vienna following the battle of Wagram, was heard crying for help late one night. When his aides rushed to his call the great soldier was discovered in his room half-dressed, and sweating profusely as he lunged with his sword at a cat hiding behind a tapestry on the wall.

Cat clocks

It is a scientifically proven fact that cats' eyes will only shine in the dark if there is some light present. In a totally black room old Sooty will be invisible. This ability of cats' eyes to reflect light, and for the pupil to dilate and contract according to the brightness of the surroundings, has been used to man's advantage in the past. Apparently in rural China it used to be the custom on cloudy days to look at a cat's eyes to tell the time. As noon approaches and the light becomes more intense the pupil gradually contracts until it is a perpendicular hair-line. After midday it slowly dilates again. Be this as it may, and assuming that your average oriental cat doesn't object to having its eyes peered into every five minutes, it could be quite useful — but what happens about British Summer Time?

Cat hotels

It seems these days that no end of extravagance is permissible in indulging the whims of one's pets, and various high-class hostelries seem to spring up regularly from time to time, advertising waterbeds for cats, pedicures and so forth. The first such institute on record was established in Philadelphia and con-

sisted of rooms decked out with three storeys of shelves with soft rugs and could accommodate 100 cats each summer. A few aristocratic cats could have rooms to themselves and their own personal hairdresser, but all would eat together and have their own plates on the dining table — a typical Sunday lunch would consist of meat soup, codfish, shrimps and mackerel, washed down with fresh milk and ice-water.

A novel variant on this theme was introduced by the Anderson House Hotel in Wabasha, Minnesota. Human guests at this hotel could actually hire a cat for company for an hour, an evening or even the night. Ten cats were kept by the owner, John Hall, and visitors could book **Morris**, **Sydney**, **Tiger**, **Aloyisius** etc. in advance at a fixed rate with food and litter provided and tidied away by the maid.

TWINS AND MULTIPLES

Ace, Deuce & Trey — One-, two-, and three-spotted playing cards.

Adam & Eve — For cats that are always in the garden.

Addison & Steele — Members of the Kit-cat Club and founders of *The Spectator*.

Antony & Cleopatra — Noble lovers.

Athos & Porthos — For two great mouse-queteers! If you have two more why not call them **Aramis** and **D'Artagnan** to complete the quartet described by Alexandre Dumas.

Auster, Boreas, Zephyr & Eurus — Greek names for the four winds.

Bangers & Mash — For a brown and a white cat?

Beaumont & Fletcher — A creative double act, after the Renaissance playwrights.

Belshazar (or Balthazar), Melchior & Caspar — The Bible's Three Wise Men.

Bonnie & Clyde — After the two bank-robbers glamorized by Warren Beatty and Faye Dunaway in the film of the same name. For two tearaway cats who always seem to be where they shouldn't be.

Box & Cox — Box is out all night and Cox is out all day, after the characters in the J.B. Morton farce.

Bubble & Squeak — For two jolly mongrels.

Castor & Pollux — The twin brothers of Helen of Troy who hatched from the egg laid by Leda after being visited by Zeus in the shape of a swan. Also known as Gemini in the star formation. Perhaps for twin male cats that look into the night sky a lot.

Compo, Clegg & Foggy — After the three characters in TV's *Last of the Summer Wine.*

Coquette & Gaspard — Two cats owned by 19th-century French poet Joseph Boulmier, who have verse written about them.

Daphnis & Chloë — Two lovers in Greek mythology.

Darby & Joan — For a couple of devoted old cats.

Dido & Aeneas — The ancient queen of Carthage and her lover.

Donner & Blitzen — 'Thunder' and 'lightning' in German, and also Santa Claus's reindeer.

Dora & Dick — Two cats owned by the celebrated children's writer Frances Hodgson Burnett (1849-1924), author of *Little Lord Fauntleroy* and countless other tales. Dick was exhibited at the first cat show in New York.

Emily, Charlotte, Anne & Branwell — After the three Brontë sisters and their brother, all cat-lovers.

Esau & Jacob — For a hairy cat and a smooth one.

Faith, Hope & Charity — The inseparable three.

Flanagan & Allen — For cats that like to sing beneath arches!

Flopsy, Mopsy, Cottontail & Peter — The names of Beatrix Potter's rabbits but just as good for cats.

Fortnum & Mason — For cats fussy about their food!

Frankie & Johnny — Immortal folk-song characters.

Fred & Ginger — After the great dancing duo, Fred Astaire

and Ginger Rogers. For two playful dancing cats, one of which is ginger, the other black-and-white (top hat and tails).

Gabriel & Michael — Two archangels.

George, Harris, Jerome & Montgomery — The three men in a boat — and their dog — in Jerome K. Jerome's book.

Gin & Tonic/Ice & Slice/Whisky & Soda — Cool customers.

Gog & Magog — Two warrior kings in the New Testament.

Gonzalez, Poiccart, Manfred & Thery — Edgar Wallace's 'Four Just Men'. (*Edgar*)

Hansel & Gretel — After the hungry lost children in Grimms' fairytale.

Hector & Lysander — A pair of heroic Greeks (both male).

Hengist & Horsa — Jutish brothers who conquered Kent in the 5th century.

Holmes & Watson — For two curious cats.

Honkers & Shankers — A pair of oriental types (Hong Kong and Shanghai).

Icarus & Daedalus — A couple of high-flyers.

Jack & Mike — Two famous cats at the British Museum. Black Jack had a white bib and paws and used to sit on the desks in the Reading Room when Sir Richard Garnett was Assistant Keeper. One day Jack appeared carrying a kitten and later died. The kitten, called Mike, was adopted by the gatekeeper and lived for 20 years more and was a familiar sight to visitors.

Jeeves & Wooster — Perhaps for a silly pedigree puss and his sensible mongrel companion?

Jekkel & Jessup — Two cats in the poem 'Five Eyes' by Walter de la Mare. The fifth eye belonged to another cat, Jill, who only had one.

Jekyll & Hyde — Two identical cats — or are they?

John, Paul, George & Ringo — For a mop-haired singing quartet.

Johnson & Boswell — They go everywhere together.

Laurel & Hardy — For a right pair of jokers, one fat and one thin!

Lone Ranger & Tonto — For a black-masked white male cat and an athletic-looking brown or black, long-haired variety. After the do-gooder Wild West horseman and his Indian sidekick that rode to the sound of the *William Tell Overture* on TV. For adventurous cats that are here one minute and gone the next.

Marks & Spencer — A dependable duo.

Matthew, Mark, Luke·& John — Saintly cats.

Moppet & Mittens — Two kittens in Beatrix Potter's stories, daughters of Mrs Tabitha Twitchit and sisters to Tom Kitten. In *The Tale of Tom Kitten* they manage to lose their pinafores, having already got grass stains on them after being given strict instructions to keep them clean. For two naughty, messy cats.

Mungojerrie & Rumpelteazer — T.S. Eliot's clowning duo.

Musky & Bullwinkle — After two cats owned by the editor of this book, Louise Dixon (Bullwinkle was a cartoon moose created in 1959 by Jay Ward Productions).

Mutt & Jeff — After the two cartoon-strip characters.

Nickel & Dime — A couple of silver-greys.

Pansy, Blanche & Tinkle — Orlando the Marmalade Cat's kittens.

Parsley, Sage, Rosemary & Thyme — A fragrant foursome, Rosemary obviously a female.

Patience & Fortitude — After the two marble lions that sit outside the New York Public Library. Originally called **Lord Lenox** and **Lady Astor** after the two patrons of the library (despite the fact that both lions are male) they were finally named by Mayor Fiorello La Guardia who always ended his Sunday broadcasts with this phrase. (*Fiorello*)

Penny & Tuppence — Penny was a female leopard cub raised by Joy Adamson and described by her in *Queen of Sheba* (1980). Tuppence was a cat owned by Dame Anna Neagle. (*Anna*)

Porgy & Bess — Singing black cats.

Pete & Dud — A right pair of jokers!

Pyramus & Thisbe — The two lovers of ancient legend whose story is told in Ovid's *Metamorphoses*. Forbidden to meet, they talk through a chink in a wall but one day, chased by a lion, Thisbe drops her veil. Pyramus finds this, thinks she is dead and stabs himself. Thisbe then returns and kills herself with his sword, and the nearby mulberry bush has born blood-red fruit ever since. Pyramus and Thisbe were also two of Cardinal Richelieu's many cats.

Quixote & Panza/Sancho — After the Cervantes characters.

Rhubarb & Custard — Rhubarb is the baseball team's cat in the satirical novel of the same name by H. Allen Smith on which the 1951 movie starring Ray Milland was based. (The part of the cat was played by double-Oscar-winner Orangey — see *Screen Cats*.) Custard, by contrast, is the purple cartoon cat that features in *Roobarb and Custard*, the animated TV series first shown on British TV in 1974 (here Roobarb is a dog).

Rodgers & Hammerstein — Another musical combination.

Romeo & Juliet — There's always one missing ('Wherefore art thou, Romeo?').

Romulus & Remus — For two cats that founded empires. Romulus and Remus were the twins suckled by a she-wolf

in Roman legend and Romulus became the founder of Rome itself.

Rosenkrantz & Guildenstern — The courtiers who always appear together in *Hamlet*.

Salt & Pepper — For two perfectly matched cats, one light, one dark.

Samson & Delilah — For two long-haired cats, or (as later in the Bible story), for a short-haired male and his partner.

Solomon & Sheba — A couple of biblical types.

Sonny & Cher — An affectionate pair.

Sooty & Sweep — Two black cats.

Starsky & Hutch — After the adventurous plain-clothes detectives in the popular US TV series. For two male cats, one fair, one dark-haired, who are both inquisitive and race about a lot.

Tango & Samba — Two Latin American dances for two slinky cats. In the 1930s Winston Churchill owned a cat called Tango at Chartwell who was included in a famous portrait of Churchill and his wife by Sir William Nicholson.

Toulouse, Marie & Berlioz — Duchess's kittens in Disney's *The Aristocats*.

Tristan & Isolde — Another romantic couple from olden times. Tristan (or Tristram), the nephew of King Mark of Cornwall, fell in love with his uncle's bride after they mistakenly drank a love potion. For a male Cornish Rex and his queen.

Tweedledum & Tweedledee — After the identical twin schoolboys in Lewis Carroll's *Through the Looking-Glass*, and two brother cats that lived at Amen Corner, London, with the scholar and writer Canon Henry Parryn Liddon (1828-90).

Twiggy & Shrimp — For two skinny but fashionable cats, after the two famous models of the 1960s, Twiggy and Jean

Shrimpton. Twiggy is also the name of one of Zoë Stokes's cats. (*Jean*)

Victoria & Albert — A couple of prudish types that don't appear at all amused?

Winston, Franklin & Joe — The Big Three, after Churchill, Roosevelt and Stalin. (*Stalin*)

Yin & Yang — The two complementary principles of Chinese philosophy. Yin is the negative, dark and feminine. Yang positive, bright and masculine. Their interaction is supposed to maintain the harmony of the universe. For two oriental cats.

Zadig & Candide — The names of Elinor Glyn's two cats, called after Voltaire's fictional heroes. (*Elinor*)

Books For Cat Lovers

The Cat Hall of Fame:
Imaginary Portraits and Profiles of the World's Most Famous Felines
by Terri Epstein and Judy Epstein Gage;
Illustrated by Roger Roth

Collected here for the first time ever are delightful full-color reproductions of the portraits of the esteemed felines who line the walls of the Cat Hall of Fame - along with their biographies - including William Shakespurr, David Litterman, Cats Domino and Pablo Picatso.

Full-color hardcover $14.95   (#72254)

The Cat Name Companion:
Facts and Fables to Help You Name Your Feline
by Mark Bryant

In this compendium of all things cat, the author looks at legendary cats, literary cats, historical cats, screen cats, and cats of the famous, and lists over 2,000 names, each with its derivation and explanation. The perfect source for finding that perfect name!

Illustrated paperback $8.95   (#51671)

Children's Letters to Socks:
Kids Write to America's First Cat
Edited by Bill Adler

Letters written by real children to ther Clintons' cat, along with humorous illustrations! "Dear Socks: Do you ever meow at cabinet meetings?" "Dear Socks: Who chases mice in the White House? You or the F.B.I.?" "Dear Socks: Do you have any brothers or sisters? My brother lives with us and it's great!

Illustrated hardcover $9.95   (#72221)

Petted by the Light:
The Most Profound and Complete Feline Near-Death Experiences Ever
by Patrick R. Tobin & Christine R. Doley

Near-Death is not just for humans! A Mew Age has dawned on America. following hot on the paws of the testimonials of dozens of people who have been embraced by the light. Here, in an unprecedented compendium, cats share their tales of the afterlife, replete with catnip gardens, oceans of cream, and a Sahara Desert's worth of kitty litter.

Illustrated hardcover $9.95   (#72314)

25 Ways to Cook a Mouse:
for the Gourmet Cat
by Orson Bean

Here's a one-of-a-kind gourmet cookbook that teaches cat lovers how to prepare the cat's most adored food: mouse. Tasteful cats everywhere will purr and paw for Mousetail Soup, Ratwurst in Beer, Southern Fried Mouse and other delectable dishes.

Illustrated hardcover $9.95 (#72199)

And One for Dog Lovers—
Do Dogs Need Shrinks?
What to Do When Man's Best Friend Misbehaves
by Peter Neville

Combining the wisdom of Sigmund Freud and the know-how of Barbara Woodhouse, here is canine Psych 101 taught by a warm-hearted pet bevaior expert. He offers solutions for every doggie mishap, including unstoppable car chasing to separation anxiety to dilemmas involving sex, eating and housebreaking.

paperback $12.95   (#51332)